Oscar Niemeyer: Works in Progress

By the same author:

LE CORBUSIER, ARCHITECT, PAINTER, WRITER, 1948. Macmillan, New York

THE WORK OF OSCAR NIEMEYER, 2nd edition, 1954. Reinhold, New York

STAMO PAPADAKI

Oscar Niemeyer: Works in Progress

REINHOLD PUBLISHING CORPORATION, NEW YORK

Contents

	Page
Foreword	7
Notes on Brazilian Architecture by Oscar Niemeyer	11
PART I: IN THE SCALE OF A SUBCONTINENT	17
Quintadinha Apartments	18
Copan Building	40
Governor Kubitscheck Building	44
Hospital Sul America	52
Montreal Building	60
Bank Mineiro de Producao	64
PART II: FORM—STRUCTURE—FORM	67
Architect's House	68
Cavanelas House	78
Modern Art Museum, Caracas	82
Hotel at Diamantina	100
Julia Kubitscheck School	104
Air Depot at Diamantina	110
Club at Diamantina	112
Chapel	116
Service Station	118
Club Libanez	122

	Page
São Paolo Exposition Center	125
The Buildings: Hall of States	134
Hall of Nations	140
Hall of Industry	142
Auditorium and Pavilion of the Arts	150
Secondary School, Belo Horizonte	154

PART III. TASKS — 159

Housing, Air Center	160
Headquarters for the Foundation Vargas	168
Berlin Housing	170
Corumbá School	178
Miranda House	180
Pigmatari House	182
De Lima House	186
Television Station	188

Foreword

In 1950 we presented in the *Work of Oscar Niemeyer* the development of a young architect, from his early projects through his formative years, following as close a chronological order as it was deemed necessary. It could be assumed now that the maturity of the middle work of Niemeyer and the rather short span which is covered here—from 1950 to 1956—should make a chronological sequence unimportant. It is less a question of following a continuous growth than of witnessing a responsible statement which must be taken on its own grounds and in the light in which it develops. And, this statement is of a highly lyrical content.

Lyricism is not the prerequisite of youth. No one, when young, is allowed to say or to say much. Le Corbusier designed first the "Citrohan"—a dwelling unit for mass production—before he built the house for Jaoul, 1922 and 1952. However lyricism is primarily a presence, a manifestation and an engagement of a presence, and the strong, the irresistible desire to express such an engagement. This is the poet's condition, but, for a builder, it will be necessary to by-pass the possible and to enter the field of all the co-possibles. It should be an activity which goes in depth, into the twilight of the consciousness where the

7

1936. Project for a multistory residence.

1950. Housing.

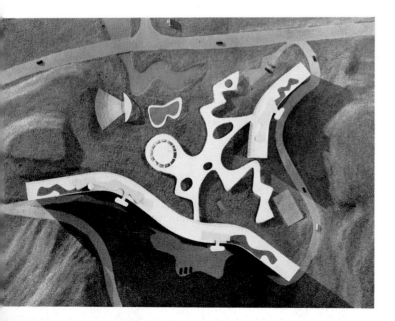

1952. Variation on the Quitandinha super block.

imaginary overshadows data and programs, all the components of an arbitrary reality which is presented in the form of formidable barriers to confound the noviciate. The answer must be a direct one but it should come from a series of depths: Jean Ducasse must completely disappear into the person of Lautreamont in order to achieve a greater reality.

When Auguste Perret developed the exterior walls of the garage at the Rue de Ponthieu (1905) he revealed the possibilities of a great heritage in revitalizing a worn-out architecture; his was the result of a high erudition which can only guide materials and static forces to a secondary plane and allow visual and virtual elements to coexist unobtrusively and with serenity. But Perret was an architect-savant, perhaps the last one of a long lineage which should include Christopher Wren. When Guarino Guarini burst his domes into flaming particles, that was the manifestation of an all-present faith, a faith very much of the day; his attitude towards the divine had no claim on the attitude which existed at the times of the cathedral nor was it expressed with the ponderous geometry of his immediate predecessors. In bypassing structural idioms, forms of data and habits of dogma, Guarini has relegated to us a very moving lyrical statement. And architecture of a purely lyrical content is rare. It antagonizes all accepted criteria, all conventional methods of evaluation; it contradicts the modesty of the average practitioner who achieves with a great deal of pain the compromise between budgets, availability of skills and materials, the problem of public acceptance and his own gloom. Lyrical exuberance is not or does not appear to be necessarily humble; it could, on the contrary, as in the *Leaves of Grass*, become aggressively fiery.

In 1954 a British architectural magazine* presented a "Report on Brazil" in which the opinions of visiting architectural ranks were exposed in length. This is a very valuable document to the extent that it reveals architectural thinking in mid-century—just some twenty-five-odd years after the era of the great emancipation and the "Esprit Nouveau." We learn here when, where and who invented, a) the glass wall, b) the "free" form, c) the brise soleil, d) the stilts, e) etc.; that all these items are part of the immediate architectural speech form; that all there is left for the designer to do now is to learn the rules of the gram-

---

*The Architectural Review, October 1954, London. It would be fair to praise here the editors' effort in presenting to their readers eyewitnesses' impressions of Brazil. In spite of this worthy gesture, Brazil remains still "that vast and legendary glass tower off the coast of Galway."

mar as they are established. And Brazilian architects were found, according to the same report, to abuse grammar without fully comprehending its rules and to subtract "social aspects of architecture" from their buildings. It is true, however, that a Japanese architect, Hiroshi Ohye, was able to detect and express with words the "state of exuberance" which exists in Brazil.

Now, why will such exuberance not make an ideal climate for architecture? This question should have been at the basis of any attempt at serious evaluation of Brazilian buildings; it was assumed, instead, that our world must be a grey one, our problems average and our language conforming to the style of financial reports. The distress resulting from the impact of such exuberance —an exuberance never itself mentioned elsewhere in the report—permeates every criticism and every comment; and it is exuberance which became the real evil spirit, the villain behind the scenes. We could only hope that such an attitude was the result of a passing postwar fatigue and of the emotional impasses that this fatigue had created.

The rights to lyricism cannot be clothed with grammatical canons, and the polyvalence of architecture does not make it necessarily suitable to vivisection: "social aspects," economic, technological, etc. Remaining an integral part of the elan vital, architecture must draw equally upon man's latest makings as well as upon man's ancestral rites. This is the reason for what Dr. S. Giedion calls the continuity of man's emotional expressions in the visual arts, from the cave paintings to the present. The findings of the new psychology in depth, the current desire to implement humanity in a continental scale and the growing understanding of aspirations in terms of global regions, rather than in sizes of parochial units alone, will further enhance the chances for an exuberant, even heroic, architecture. The progressive dematerialization that we witness in the recent buildings of Niemeyer can hardly be seen as the result of a technological penury; on the contrary, it points the dawn of a still greater lyrical outburst.

Washington, Connecticut, 1956.

possibilidades técnicas

arquitetura

condições sociais

Notes on Brazilian Architecture

by Oscar Niemeyer

Some of our architects have been possessed by a strange urge. Although they know well that modern Brazilian architecture enjoys an undeniable prestige, these architects suddenly confront us with problems. They are divided into two schools of thought. The first is represented by those who are impressed with evolutionary theories and strive for "an architecture based on the traditions and culture of our people." The second is made up of those who show alarm over the low quality of our present day construction and demand more simple and realistic building methods. We respect the opinions of both groups; the first because it is sincere and wishes for a solution which appears to be more natural and the second because it sounds extremely logical. Both groups, however, are exiling to a secondary plan the most serious and urgent needs for a local building program.

In addition to the native criticisms we have also the adverse opinions of some of our colleagues who have visited us from abroad. Their criticisms of Brazilian architecture cannot always be justified. It seems that they do not use the same measure—severe and objective—when they deal with their own projects as when they are examining ours. The fact that they work with powerful industries which demand more simple solutions so as to take advantage of prefabricated assemblies and systems of standardization and their lack of knowledge of our actual conditions of work which are entirely different from their own, may explain some of their tension and uneasiness in regard to Brazilian architecture.

Our modern architecture reflects the social contradictions in which we live and in which it has developed. Presented to clients not interested in problems of a general building economy and to a governmental body that shies from plans of national dimensions and from large scale construction projects, our architecture is forced to make improvisation its basic element.

Under those circumstances we practised our profession for twenty years, designing houses for the middle class, government structures, office buildings and apartment houses. Some of these buildings are often appreciated from a design point of view but they always reflect the social disequilibrium of the country with a majority of its citizens living in the most miserable quarters. The great variety of forms that is seen in our architecture stems from the lack of an effective social and economic basis. The absence of a large building industry with prefabricated assemblies and parts further encourages the development of a wealth of individualistic architectural forms and solutions. Thus, what appears ludicrous to someone looking from the outside to us is a necessity dictated by present day conditions. For this reason we refuse to strive for a more rigid and impersonal architecture—the European tendency, the result of applying industrial techniques—as we refuse to pretend that there exists a basis for "social architecture." To do the contrary would mean to accept an architectural poverty, to deprive our architecture of what it has that is fresh and creative or to instil

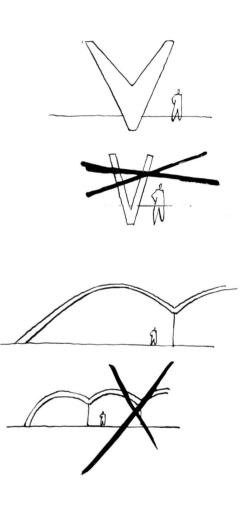

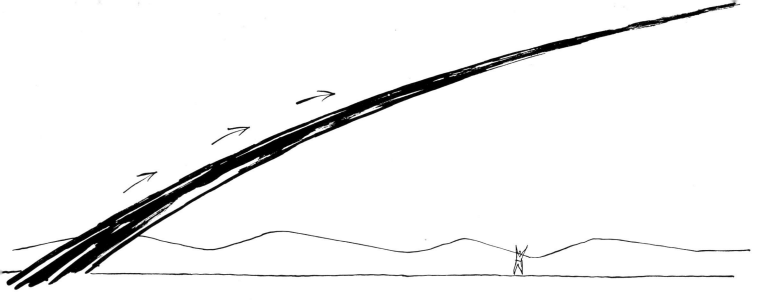

"Conquest of space, a free environment, is the constant pre-occupation of architecture. And the reinforced concrete allows generous realizations with a variety of new and unexpected forms."

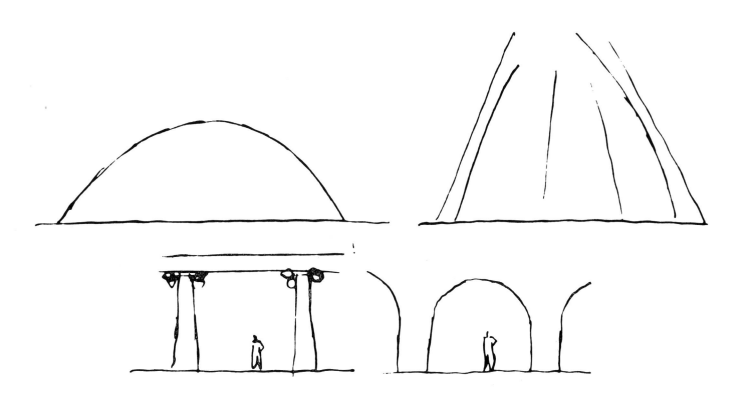

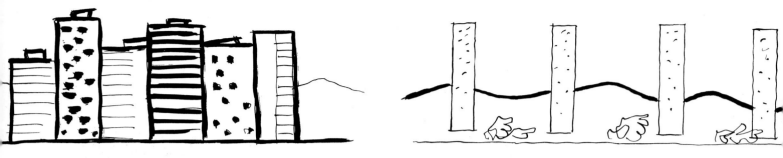

"Skyscrapers, high walls which hide behind them the mountains, hills, beaches and trees, the essential elements that nature gave us, present the most serious urban problem."

in our buildings political demagoguery. We made the choice of preserving in our architecture whatever native and spontaneous characteristics it has, of speculating imaginatively with the methods of construction in use and we hoped to remain worthy of the prestige which Brazilian architecture retains in the contemporary world.

Credit for this must be given to Lucio Costa——a major figure in our modern movement. Since its beginning Costa has worked for an architecture which could combine functional and emotional qualities. His work with the national monuments brought to light all the rational and plastic aspects of vernacular buildings with the resulting effect of disciplining and simplifying our modern forms. Furthermore, Costa strengthened our position in regard to tradition: we refuse to imitate but we wish to maintain the same structural honesty which always characterized our colonial architecture.

On opposite page: preliminary plan for Marine City, a complete urban settlement with industry (right), civic center and office buildings (left, center), large multiple dwelling units indicated with slightly curved forms, and four neighborhood units of one-family houses, A, B, C, D. Each unit is divided into two parts by an area given over to pedestrian traffic where schools, shops, clubs, sport facilities are located. There is provision for three types of traffic: high speed, local and pedestrian. Associate Architects: Nauro Esteves, Jose Reis and Lopes da Silva.

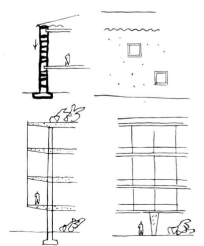

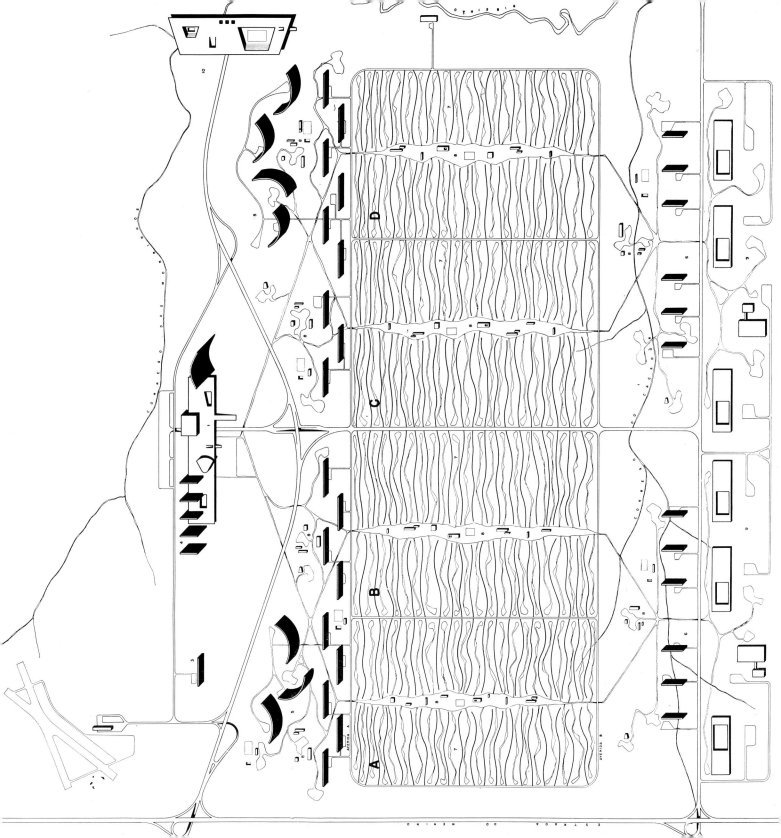

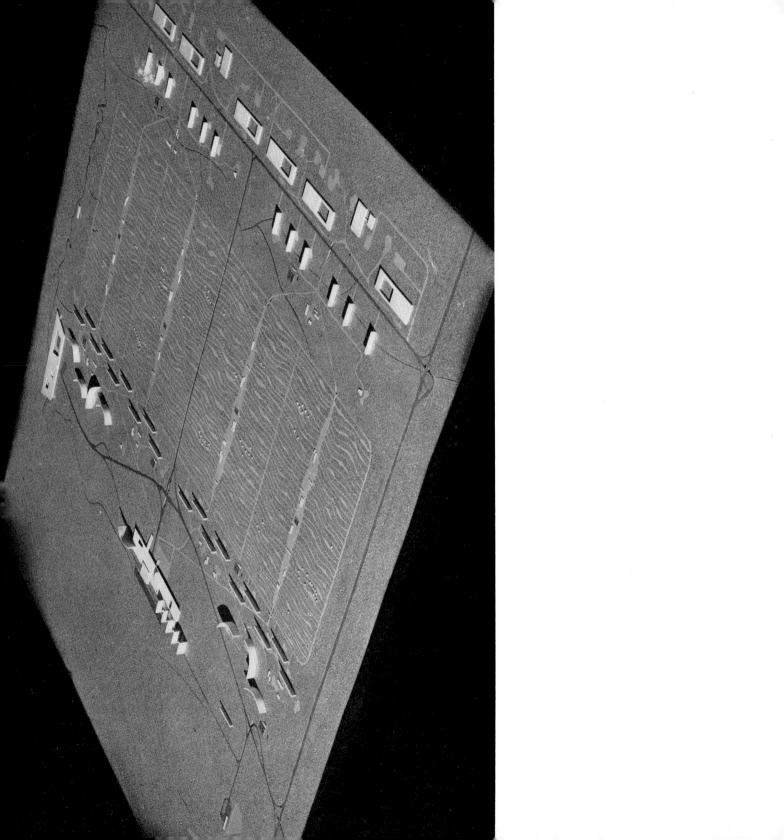

PART I

in the scale of a subcontinent

The new work of Oscar Niemeyer presented in this book—from 1950 to 1956—is divided into three parts for the sole purpose of obtaining a visual simplification. Since this is not a division in depth but rather a grouping by association, some overlapping is to be found among parts. Buildings presented in this section are characterized by their size: that the size is an aspect of what was called the "new giantism" or the result of an effort to implement efficiently a subcontinent of the dimensions of Brazil should be of secondary importance; a building, by the way it takes possession of its quantity of space, is not only an activity but is also a reality with a life and a system of reason of its own.

1950. Quitandinha, apartment hotel at Petropolis. Photography: R. Landau. This is, perhaps, the boldest single building project in our time. Over a quarter of a mile long, a true one-building town, it joins the family of the world's largest dams and dominates the landscape in competition with such natural elements as mountains and gorges. Proposed for the resort town of Petropolis, the vacation grounds of the Cariocas (the people of Rio de Janeiro), the hotel contains 5,700 dwelling units of five basic types in

33 stories. A shopping center of 200 units, sport, amusement, health, and medical facilities are included in sheltered or open, terraced grounds on the first floor and two mezzanines. For comparison of the basic dimensions: Quitandinha, length: 1,380 ft., width: 54 ft., height: 394 ft. Unité d' Habitation at Marseilles by Le Corbusier, length: 541 ft., width: 79 ft., height: 184 ft. Pyramid of Cheops (Khufu), base: 755 ft., height: 482 ft. Kentucky Dam (TVA); length: 1,788 ft., height: 160 ft.

19

Aerial view of the model shows the island where the building is situated. This island, outlined by the access road, is given over to pedestrian traffic. Four semidetached elevator towers on the convex side of the building

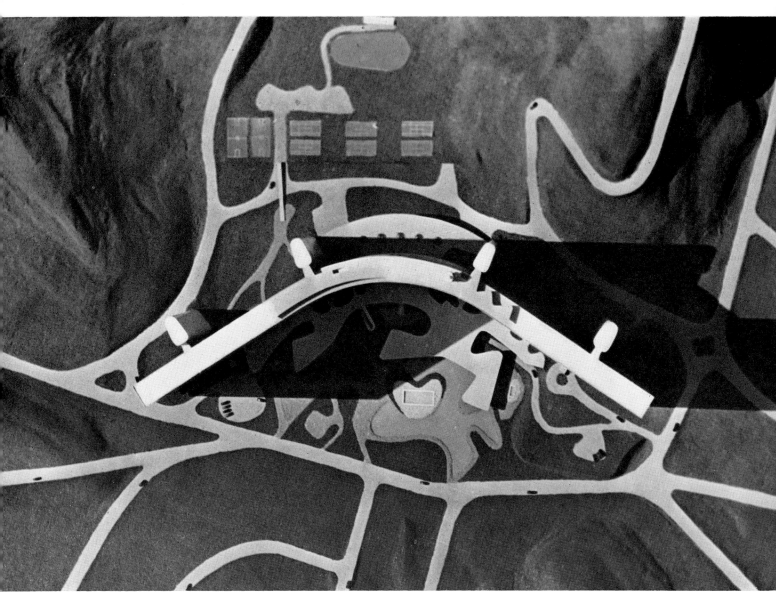

provide vertical communication allowing a maximum walking distance to and from the elevators of 170 ft. All maintenance and service traffic takes place between the two center towers.

Here and on the following pages are illustrated the basic thoughts which conditioned the design of Quitandinha. Preference was given to a solution with a single super-building rather than to a maze of gridiron blocks or to a number of buildings of more modest dimensions (sketches right). The section below shows the key to the adopted solution: a dwelling unit with cross-ventilation obtained by staggered floor levels and serviced by an interior corridor located at an intermediate level. The hotel "Latitude 43" at Saint Tropez designed by Pingusson during the early 1930's presented a similar solution. The problem there was to secure for the guests a view of the Mediterranean on the north side of the building together with adequate sunshine from the southern exposure. The accommodations for guests, however, were of the transient type, bed room and bath.

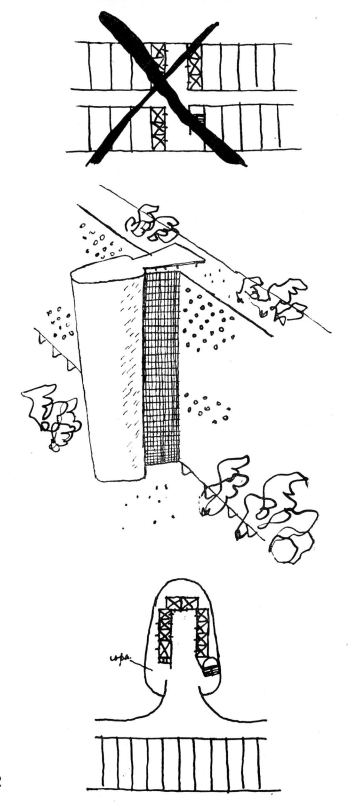

Studies of the vertical circulation: a semi-detached tower containing 10 passenger and freight elevators, emergency stairs and passenger lobby is adopted (instead of accommodating elevators between dwelling units, top

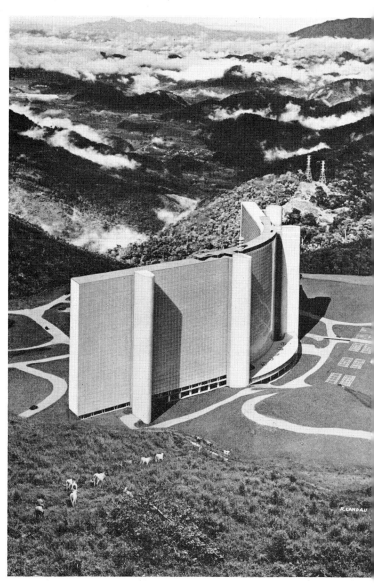

sketch). Noise and traffic related to vertical circulation offer thus a minimum disturbance to the dwellers. Sketch on opposite page indicates the servicing area between the two center elevator towers.

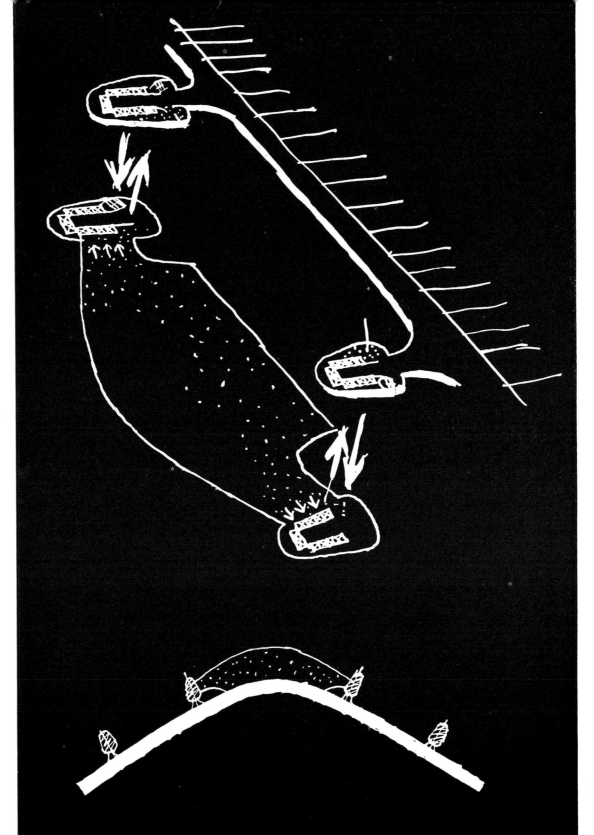

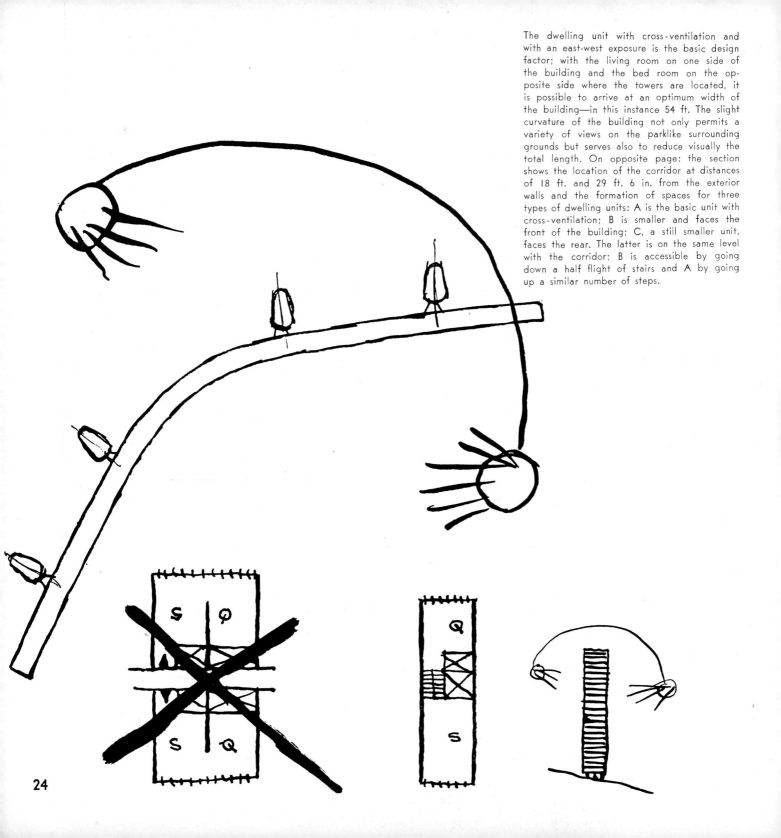

The dwelling unit with cross-ventilation and with an east-west exposure is the basic design factor; with the living room on one side of the building and the bed room on the opposite side where the towers are located, it is possible to arrive at an optimum width of the building—in this instance 54 ft. The slight curvature of the building not only permits a variety of views on the parklike surrounding grounds but serves also to reduce visually the total length. On opposite page: the section shows the location of the corridor at distances of 18 ft. and 29 ft. 6 in. from the exterior walls and the formation of spaces for three types of dwelling units: A is the basic unit with cross-ventilation; B is smaller and faces the front of the building; C, a still smaller unit, faces the rear. The latter is on the same level with the corridor; B is accessible by going down a half flight of stairs and A by going up a similar number of steps.

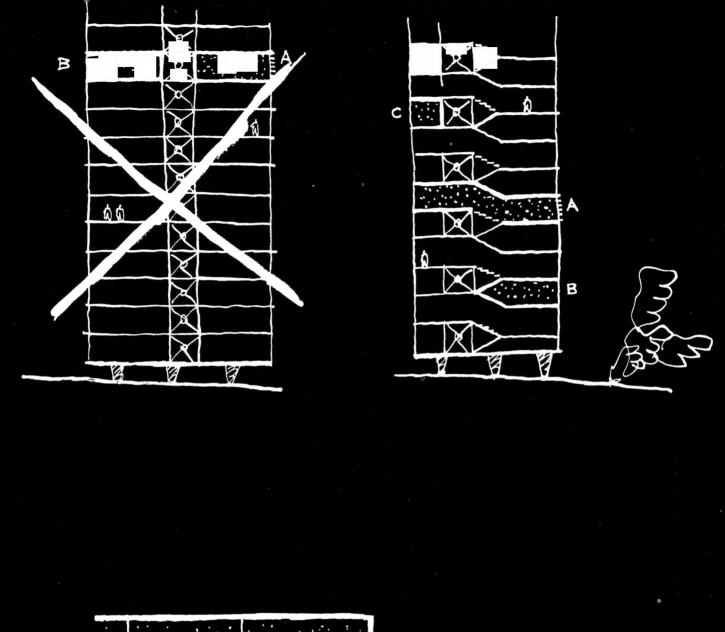

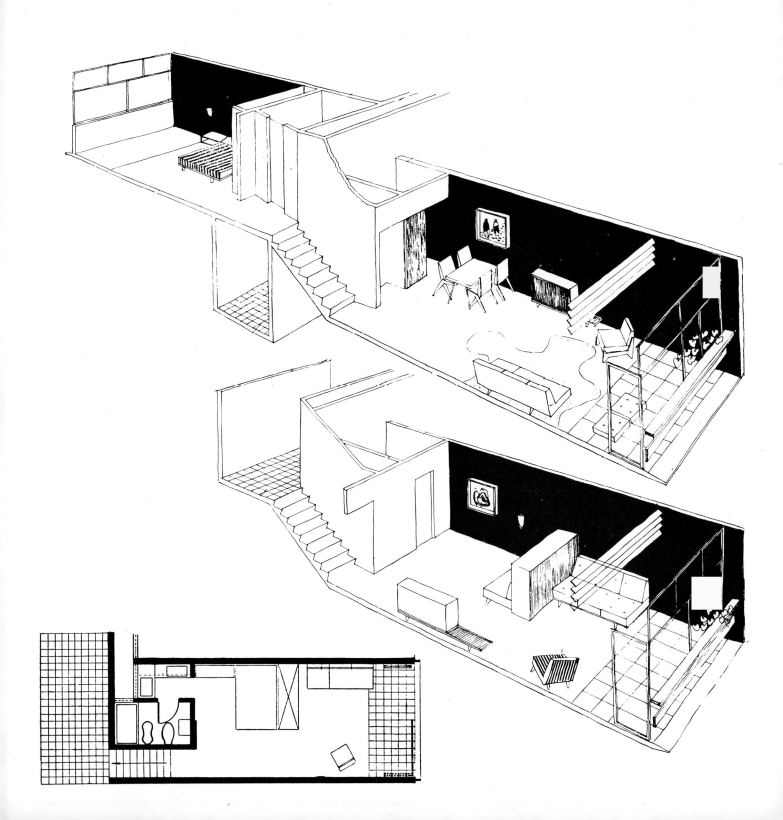

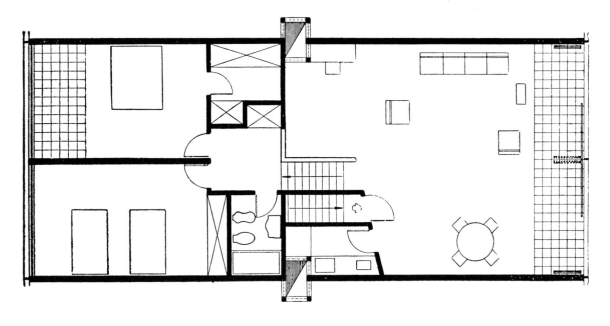

Unit plans for Quitandinha: unit A at the bottom of the page and unit 2A at the top, for the latter unit a double width of 11 ft. 6 in. is being used to accommodate a second bed room. On opposite page is the plan for unit B and, right, the plan for unit 2B. Nine steps connect the units with the corridor and the living room with the bed room. In units A and 2A the bath rooms are located above the corridor.

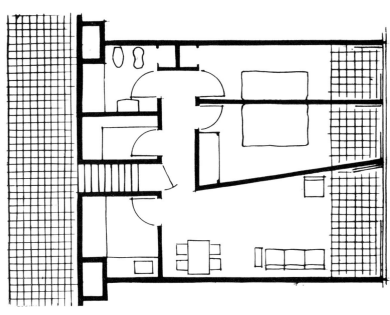

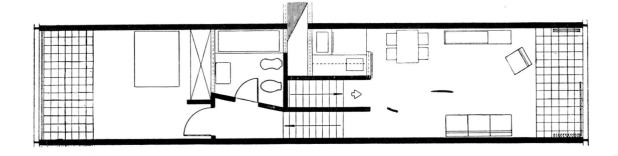

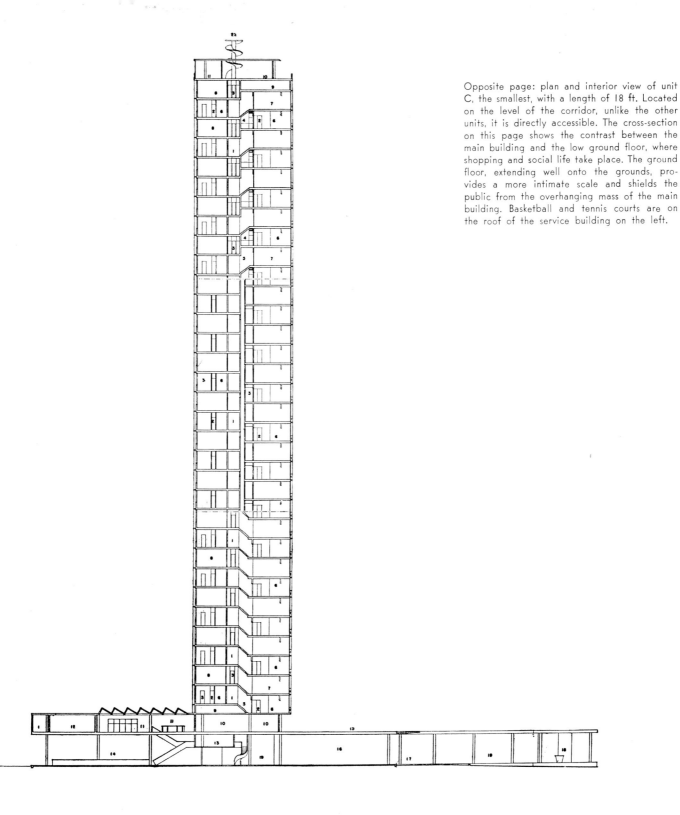

Opposite page: plan and interior view of unit C, the smallest, with a length of 18 ft. Located on the level of the corridor, unlike the other units, it is directly accessible. The cross-section on this page shows the contrast between the main building and the low ground floor, where shopping and social life take place. The ground floor, extending well onto the grounds, provides a more intimate scale and shields the public from the overhanging mass of the main building. Basketball and tennis courts are on the roof of the service building on the left.

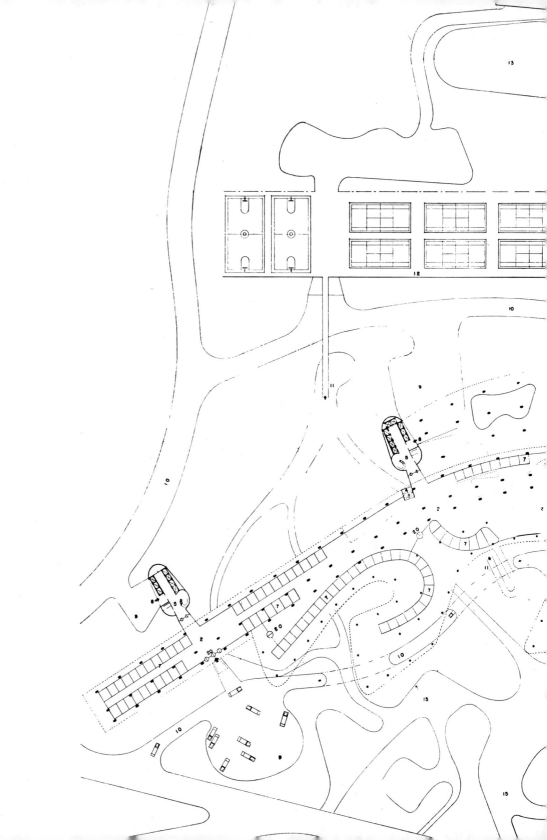

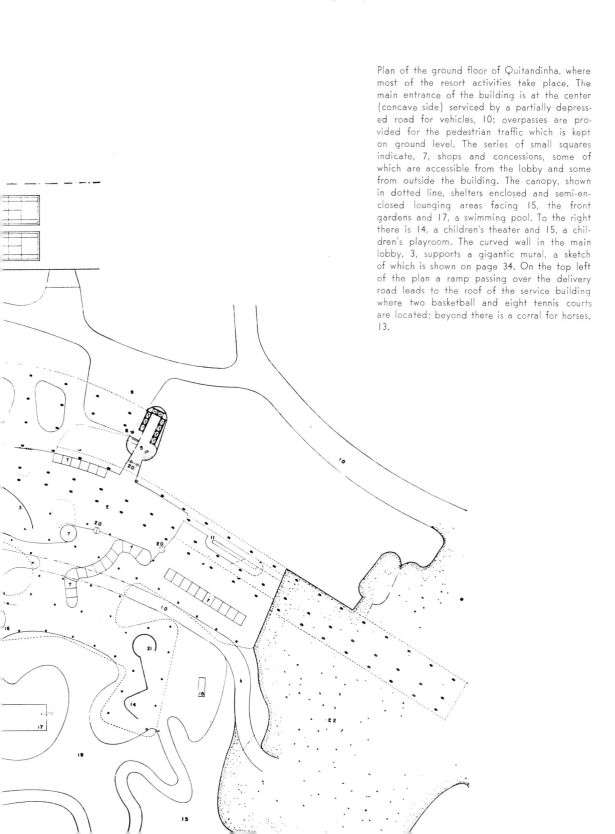

Plan of the ground floor of Quitandinha, where most of the resort activities take place. The main entrance of the building is at the center (concave side) serviced by a partially depressed road for vehicles, 10; overpasses are provided for the pedestrian traffic which is kept on ground level. The series of small squares indicate, 7, shops and concessions, some of which are accessible from the lobby and some from outside the building. The canopy, shown in dotted line, shelters enclosed and semi-enclosed lounging areas facing 15, the front gardens and 17, a swimming pool. To the right there is 14, a children's theater and 15, a children's playroom. The curved wall in the main lobby, 3, supports a gigantic mural, a sketch of which is shown on page 34. On the top left of the plan a ramp passing over the delivery road leads to the roof of the service building where two basketball and eight tennis courts are located; beyond there is a corral for horses, 13.

The ground floor is a continuous indoor-outdoor area. The sketch above shows a fragment of outdoors carefully "caged" somewhere in the main lobby behind the mural-screen. At the bottom of the opposite page there is a view of the children's theater.

Above: preliminary study for the mural in the main lobby by Aristido Portinari on a historical theme. On opposite page: a view from the bar towards the swimming pool and the small artificial lake.

The first mezzanine (plan below) covers a relatively small area close to the elevator towers. Besides I, the main desk and the managerial offices which are located here, the rest of the space is taken by services: barber shops and beauty parlors, dental and medical offices, physiotherapy rooms, etc. The second mezzanine, not shown here, occupies the area directly below the main building; it is open to the extensive terraces over the ground floor lobby and is accessible directly from the gardens through ramps. A very large dining hall about half the length of the building, a children's restaurant, reading rooms, some more sheltered lounges and additional shops occupy this area. Kitchen and food storage are located in the space between the two center elevator towers, indicated with dotted lines on the plan below.

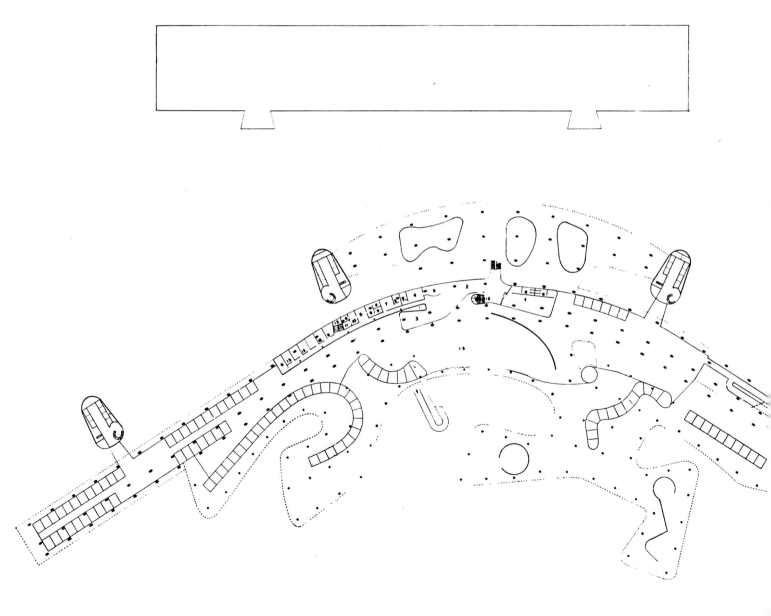

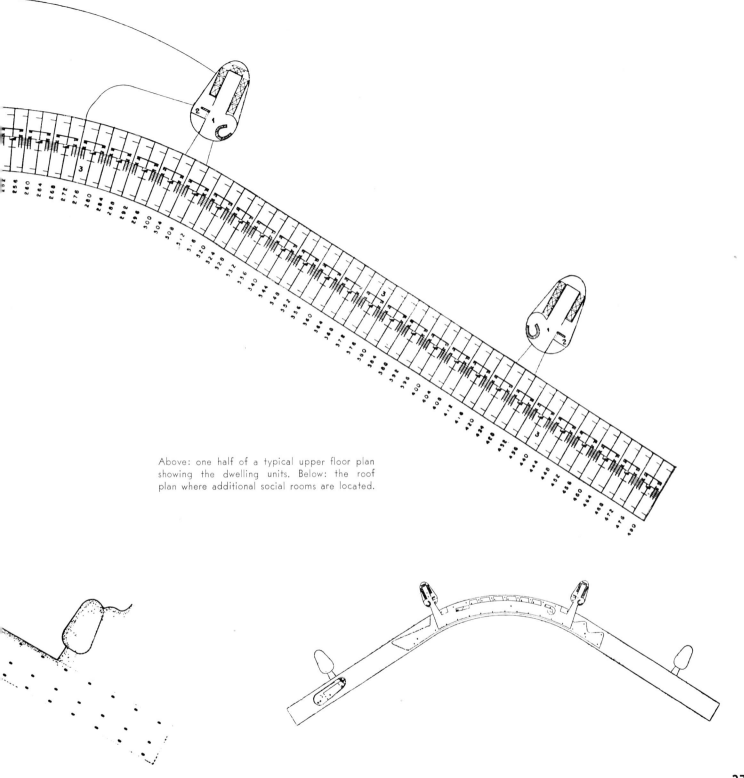

Above: one half of a typical upper floor plan showing the dwelling units. Below: the roof plan where additional social rooms are located.

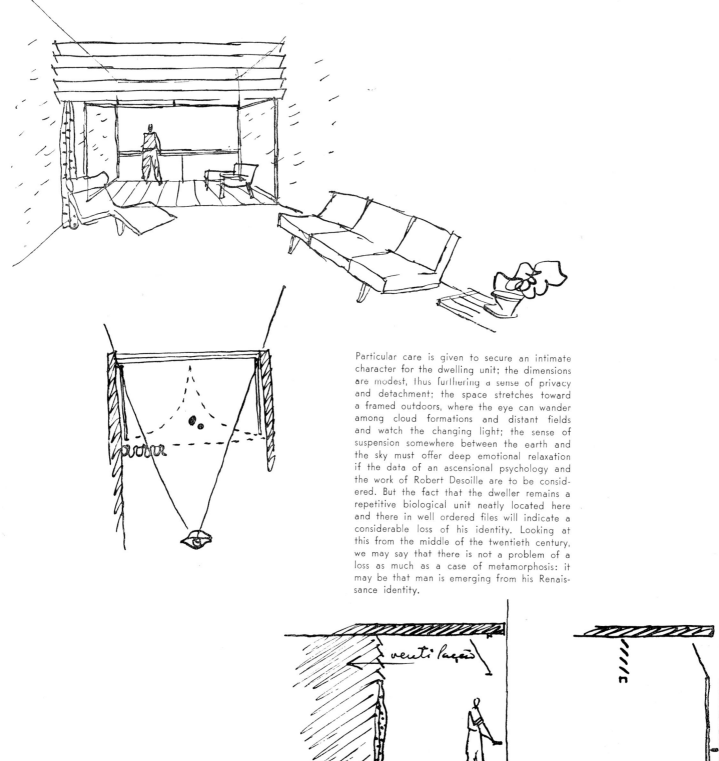

Particular care is given to secure an intimate character for the dwelling unit; the dimensions are modest, thus furthering a sense of privacy and detachment; the space stretches toward a framed outdoors, where the eye can wander among cloud formations and distant fields and watch the changing light; the sense of suspension somewhere between the earth and the sky must offer deep emotional relaxation if the data of an ascensional psychology and the work of Robert Desoille are to be considered. But the fact that the dweller remains a repetitive biological unit neatly located here and there in well ordered files will indicate a considerable loss of his identity. Looking at this from the middle of the twentieth century, we may say that there is not a problem of a loss as much as a case of metamorphosis: it may be that man is emerging from his Renaissance identity.

1951. Copan Building, São Paolo. Photography: R. Landau. The two buildings proposed for an area situated at the intersection of Avenue Ipiranga and S. Luiz Street are for a hotel (smaller building) and a cooperative apartment house (*condominio* as it is called in Brazil). This group will include a garage for 500 cars, a moving picture theater, "shopping streets" on two levels—ground and mezzanine floors, restaurants, a night club, etc. The ground floor plan, shown on this page, contains "shopping streets," the hotel lobby and the night club directly at the rear of the lobby.

41

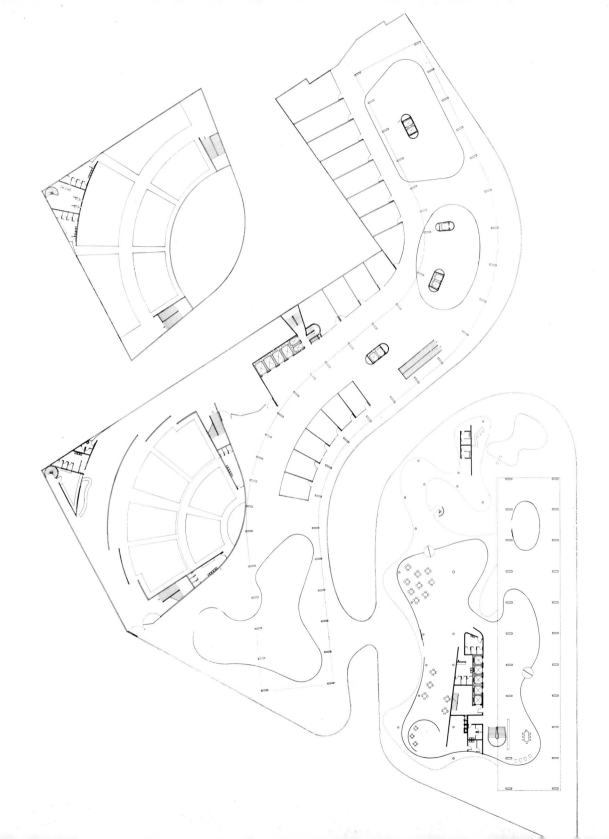

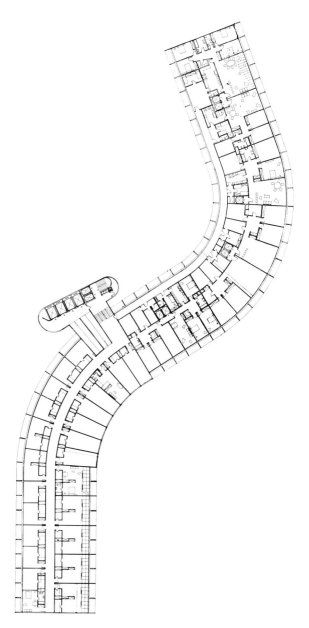

On the mezzanine floor, opposite page, which is sparingly enclosed, there are a small number of shops, a large restaurant connected with the hotel, the theater and the lobbies of the apartment house. Left: a typical floor plan of the apartment house shows a variety of apartment types. A semidetached elevator-

stairs tower serves approximately half the length of the building, and the apartments located there are accessible through a center corridor. Larger apartments are serviced by separate elevators in groups of two; an open corridor links these apartments with the central tower, providing means of emergency exit.

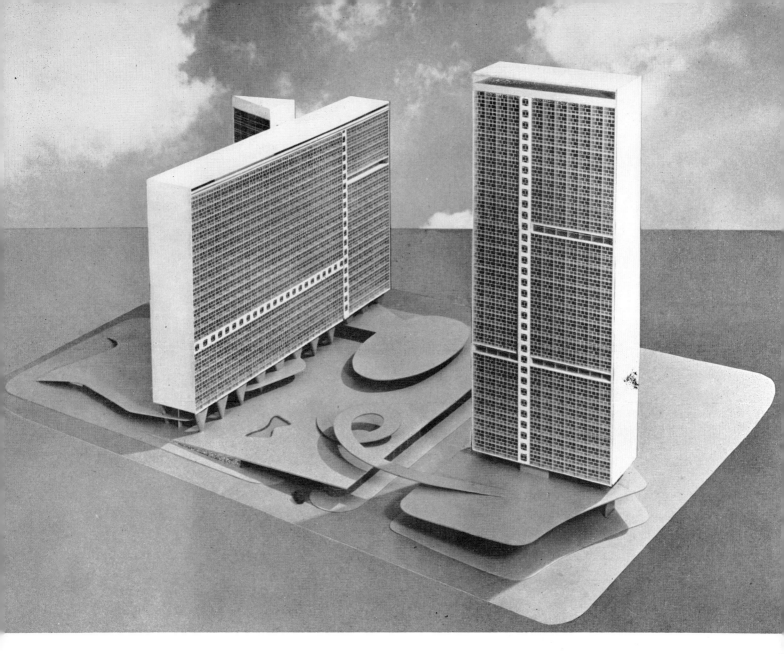

1951. Governor Kubitscheck Building, Belo Horizonte. Structural Engineer: Joaquim Cardozo. Photography: R. Landau and Marcel Gautherot. Far more complex than the Quitandinha apartments, as a program if not in size, this group of buildings is planned to provide dwelling units of a great variety of types for permanent and transient living quarters. It is named after the former Governor of the State of Minas Gerais and later President of Brazil to commemorate his effort in encouraging ad-vanced architecture and planning in his state (see *The Work of Oscar Niemeyer*, pages 71-115). The sketches illustrate the main design elements: location of the buildings so as to create a minimum obstruction of view; repetition of certain features of the façades to obtain a sense of unity; the development of bulkier stilts which, however, offer less obstruction on the pedestrian level. The lower building, being at present under construction, is further illustrated on the following pages.

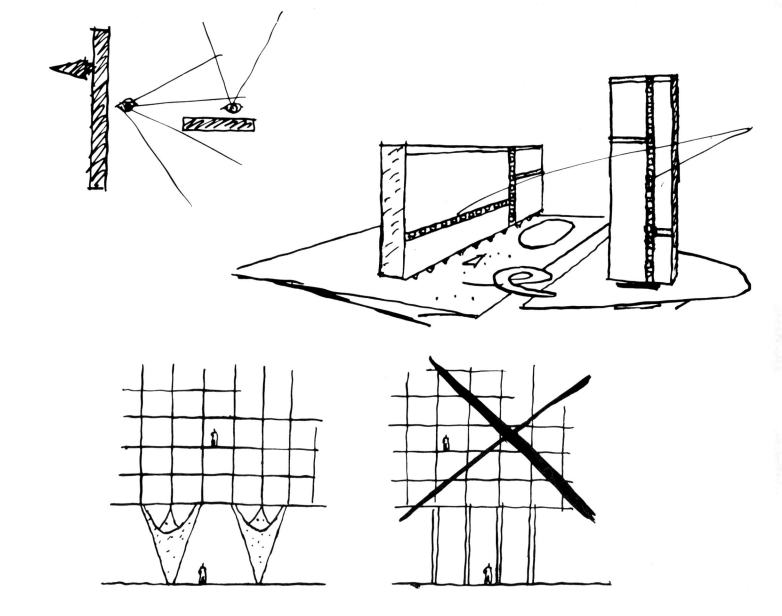

Plan of the lower level (below): 1, parking; 2, restaurant; 3, public space; 4, private road; 5, shops. Intermediate level (opposite page): 6, foyer; 7, moving picture theater; 8, air conditioning; 9, hotel lobby; 10, apartments lobby; 11, lounge; 12, service; 13, restaurant; 14, roof garden; 15, swimming pool, and, under a canopy shown with dotted lines, a refreshment stand.

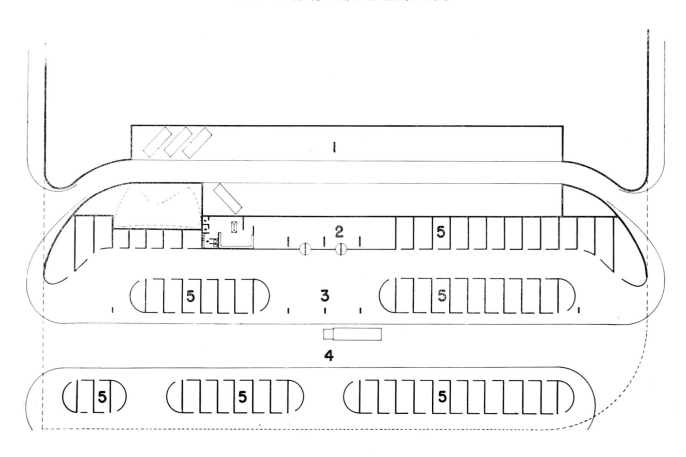

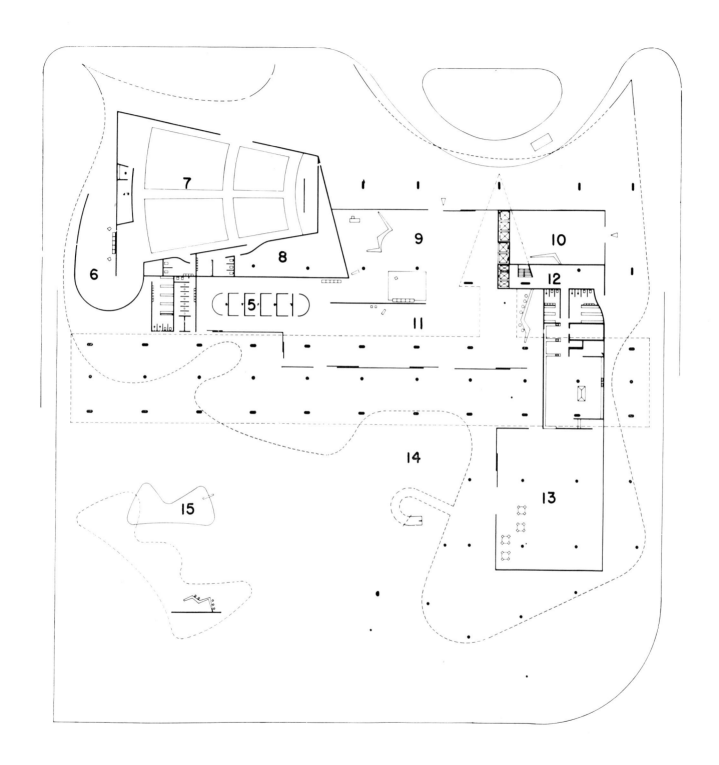

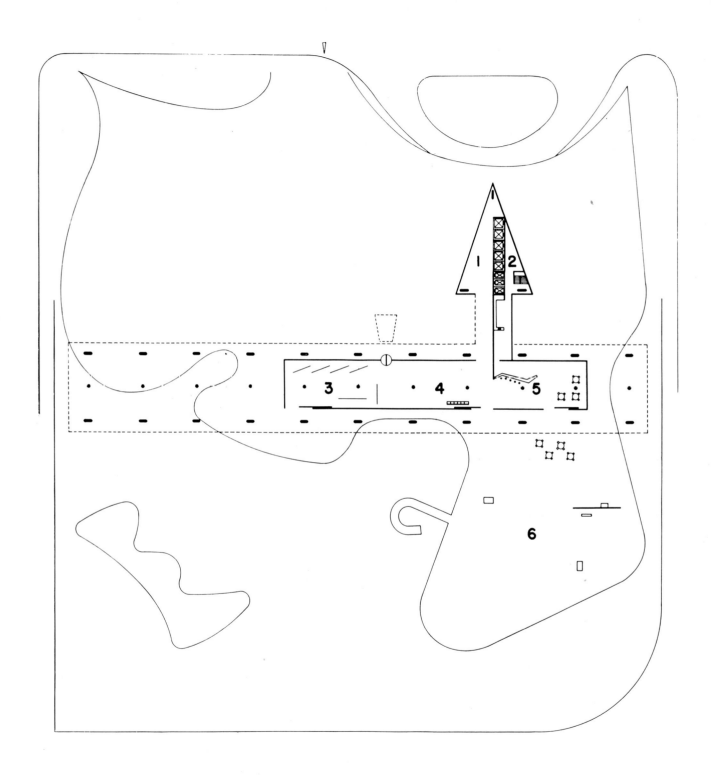

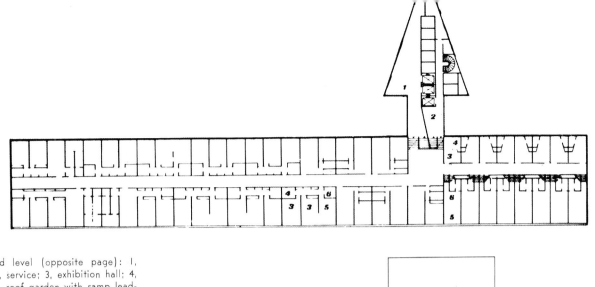

Plan of the third level (opposite page): 1, elevator tower; 2, service; 3, exhibition hall; 4, lounge; 5, bar; 6, roof garden with ramp leading to the lower level. Typical floor plan (above): 1, elevator lobby; 2, service; 4, bath room; 5, living room; 6, kitchen. Below: cross section showing the Quitandinha type of dwelling unit with staggered floor levels combined with more traditional types of apartments located on both sides of a central corridor.

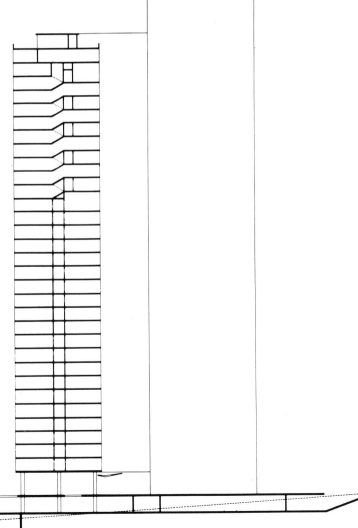

On this and on the following page are construction photographs taken in the summer of 1955: the giant stilts, the bearing walls which eliminate the need for columns and hanging beams, and the framing of the elevator tower (upper right). Each stilt supports two spans and there is the distance of one span between two consecutive stilts. The second picture from left shows a stilt with an expansion joint. The bearing walls are located between dwelling units, and, besides providing flush walls and ceilings, they have been proven to be economical in London's low cost housing designed by Tecton and in the Nantes-Rezé building by Le Corbusier. Below: plan of the top floor designed as a continuous flowing space and given over to entertainment functions: 1, entrance; 2, dance floor; 3, stage with circular stairs leading to dressing rooms above; 4, kitchen. On the left of the dancing area there is a bar and lounge; open terraces are on both ends of the floor.

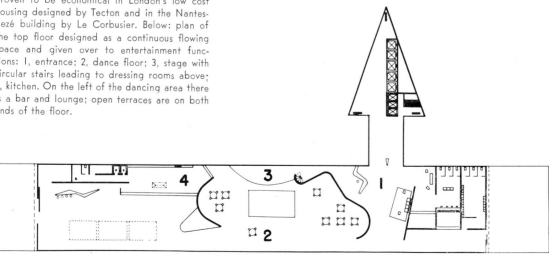

1952. Hospital "Sul America" at Rio de Janeiro. Associate Architect: Helio Uchoa. Landscape Designer: Roberto Burle Marx. Structural Engineer: Morales Ribeiro. Hospital Consultant: Dr. Leonidio Ribeiro. Photography: H. Landau and H. Barboza. This hospital with 10 floors and basement and with a capacity of 280 beds is designed to provide medical and nursing facilities for the employees of the Insurance Company "Sul America" and the Bank "Lar Brasileiro." Its main characteristics are the absence of nursing wards, each patient being

provided with a semiprivate or private room
and bath, and the elimination of the outpatient
department; services for the latter are to be
provided in local dispensaries. There are five
floors of patients' rooms, all facing an extensive park and Lake Rodrigo, and the services
are located in the rear. The small building in
the foreground is for a chapel to be erected
at a later date when the design reaches a more
final stage. V-shaped stilts on the periphery of
the building rest on piles 75 ft. deep; between
two stilts there is a standard span of approximately 25 ft. A semidetached tower provides
additional vertical communication (right).

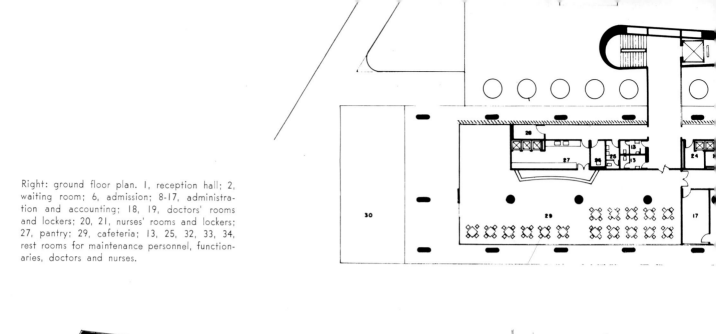

Right: ground floor plan. 1, reception hall; 2, waiting room; 6, admission; 8-17, administration and accounting; 18, 19, doctors' rooms and lockers; 20, 21, nurses' rooms and lockers; 27, pantry; 29, cafeteria; 13, 25, 32, 33, 34, rest rooms for maintenance personnel, functionaries, doctors and nurses.

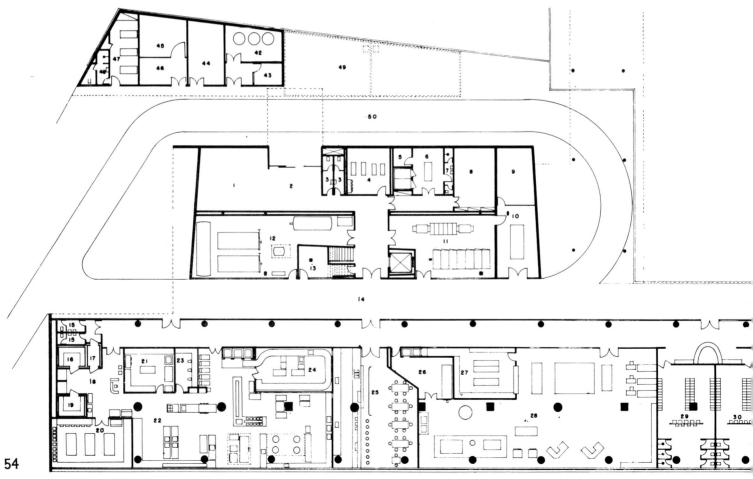

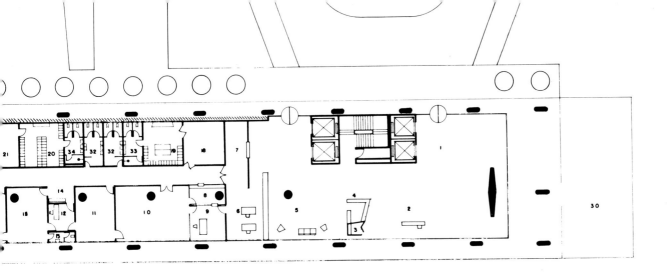

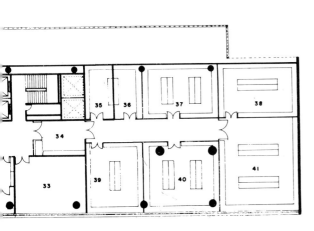

Left: basement plan. 1-8, morgue and autopsy rooms; 9-12, mechanical equipment; 14, covered passage; 20, 21, dietitians' offices; 22, kitchen; 24, dishwashing; 25, kitchen help cafeteria; 26-28, soiled and clean linen, laundry; 29, 30, lockers; 35-39, storage; 42, water filters; 44, oxygen storage; 45, 46, offices; 47, ambulance drivers' quarters; 49, underground water storage; 50, vehicular circulation.

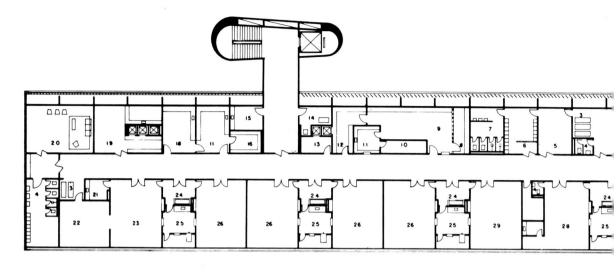

Above: 9th floor. 1, hall; 2, nurses' post; 5, surgeons' lounge; 8-12, sterilization; 22, 23, 26, 28, 29, 30, 31, specialized operating rooms; 34, postoperative recuperation room.

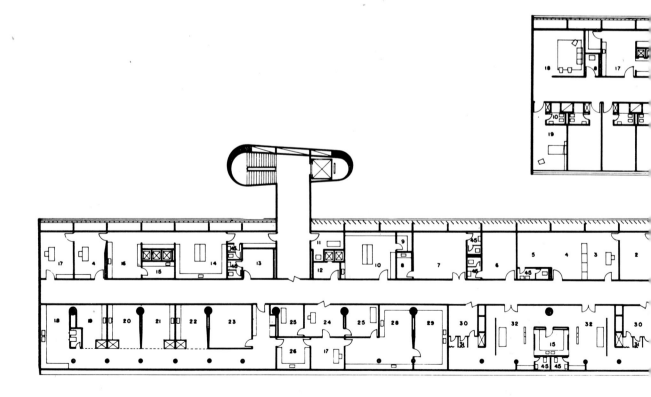

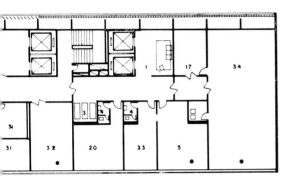

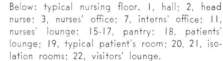

Below: typical nursing floor. 1, hall; 2, head nurse; 3, nurses' office; 7, interns' office; 11, nurses' lounge; 15-17, pantry; 18, patients' lounge; 19, typical patient's room; 20, 21, isolation rooms; 22, visitors' lounge.

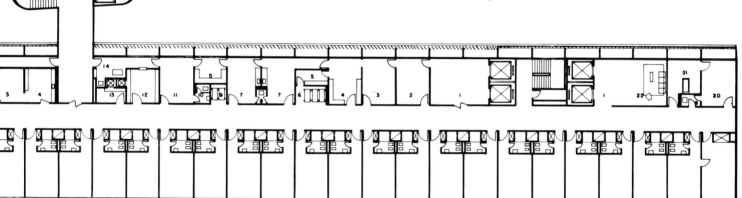

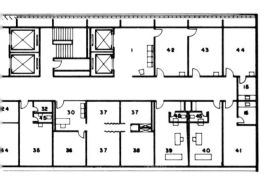

Left: 2nd floor plan providing facilities for the periodical health check-up of the employees of the insurance company. 1, 2, entrance and waiting room; 3-5, head nurse and files; 6, 13, patients' lounges; 7, doctors' lounge; 10, pharmacy; 14-16, laboratories; 17, director's office; 18-29, sterilizing room and special laboratories; 30-34, x-ray department; 36-38, physiotherapy; 39-44, specialists' offices.

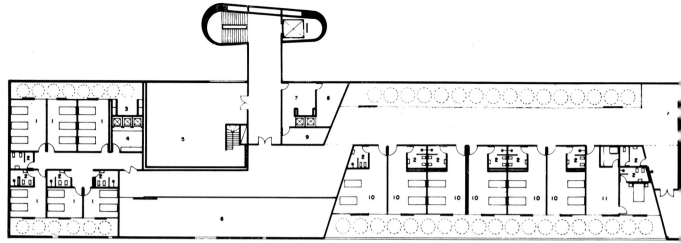

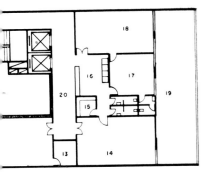

Left: 10th floor plan. 1, nurses' quarters; 2, bath rooms; 4, pantry; 5, air conditioning; 6, garden; 10, interns' quarters; 11, director's apartment; 12, board room; 14, library; 16, 17 office of the director; 18, files; 19, terrace. Below: the view of Lake Rodrigo, extending as far as the opposite shores, can be enjoyed from all patients' rooms; this picture is taken from a point halfway the length of the building. On opposite page, extreme left, is the elevation that faces the lake with six stories of patients' rooms.

1950. Montreal Building at São Paolo. Photography R. Landau. Situated at the sharp intersection of two avenues, this building consists of a ground floor and twenty stories of rentable space for offices and showrooms. The horizontal, closely spaced fins create the impression that

the Montreal is a much taller building or has a greater number of floors, thus disproving the accepted opinion that horizontal lines always are the best means to shorten a given height. There are three fins per floor, all with perforations, and the middle one divides the window into two parts. As the condition of the insolation changes around the corner, the horizontal fins are replaced with vertical, adjustable louvers.

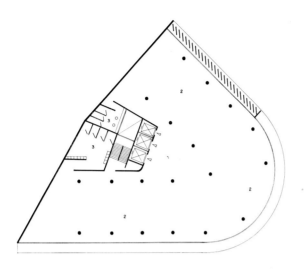

Below: Ground floor plan. 1, entrance; 2, hall; 3, shops; 4, restaurant; 5, equipment and storage; 6, bar; 7, kitchen. Above: typical floor plan. 1, hall; 2, rentable space; 3, rest rooms.

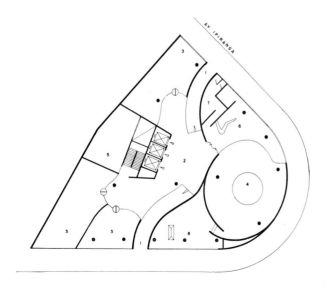

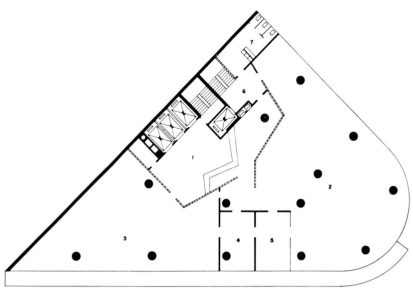

1953. Offices for the Bank "Mineiro da Producao," Belo Horizonte. Structural Engineer: W. Muller. Photography: R. Landau. Another "Flatiron" building on a triangular lot provides 12 stories of banking offices and 12 stories of rental space; banking business is conducted on the ground floor and the mezzanine. Ground floor plan (lower right): 1, ramp leading to the mezzanine; 2, main entrance to the bank; 3, entrance to the office building; 4, main banking area; 5, 6, 9 and 10, tellers' booths

and officers' desks; 11, waiting area; 12, 13, entrance, hall and elevator for the bank's personnel. This separation between public and employees' traffic is maintained on all the bank's floors. Third floor plan (upper right): 1, 6, public and employees' hall; 2, 3, general office area; 4, 5, offices of department heads. On the photograph above, showing the construction in progress, we can notice the relatively humble buildings on the party wall.

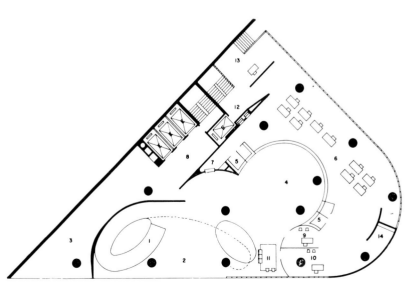

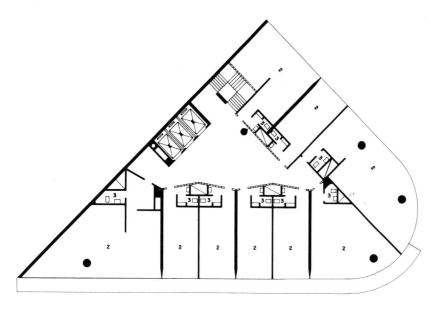

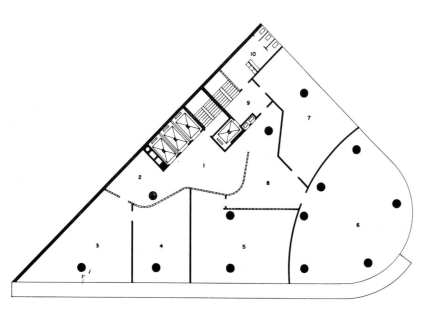

Fourth floor plan (lower left): 1, 2, public hall; 3-7, administration offices; 8, 9, employee's circulation. Typical plan for the 12th-24th floors (left) contains rental office units, each one with private wash room, reminiscent in a way of hotel suites.

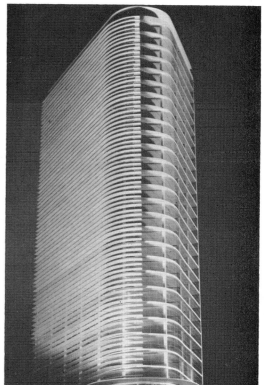

PART II

form-structure-form

Here are assembled buildings and projects of various types and sizes having, perhaps, one thing in common: the architect's preoccupation with achieving an emotional impact. This is to say that in a building, be it a house, a museum or a school, the function, the spatial economy and the directness of structure become secondary; they fade out during the process of complete metamorphosis. Terrain data, structure and function are transcended by an often unexpected form which is certainly not the result of an additive operation or of combinations and adjustments. At the present time, when accepted architectural idioms are to be found in many climates and places, it is difficult to say that this is the personal way of a designer and not a permanent acquisition of contemporary architecture. If the latter be true, then achitecture is going beyond the stage of implementing an industrial society and works again for the "emotional man" in a real Apollonian tradition.

1953. House of the architect at Canoa, Rio de Janeiro. This is the building which in 1954 created a tempest in a teapot. It was the time when a delegate from Switzerland and another one from a neighboring region were suddenly confronted with continental dimensions and strange flora and fauna while distributing ar-

chitectural medals and premiums in Brazil. Their experience as guests must have been unbearable because this house was conceived as a receiving post for the full impact of nature: from falling waters to flocks of birds of paradise, from strident color eruptions to man-swallowing vistas. And the result was thunderous. We heard about "incoherent relationship between the ground floor and . . . ," "poorly ventilated mezzanine," the lack of similarity to a "Pompeian house," up to a definition that "Art consists in making an idea as clear and objective as it can be made," obviously referring to the technique of writing military dispatches. The house was designed so as not to be an obstruction to a vista divided into front and back views, but to secure a scenic continuity. On high ground, between two steep hills, the house consists primarily of a canopy and some movable and permanent screens used with a great deal of discretion as to their number and location. A mounting path, shown in the foreground of the large picture, provides the main access.

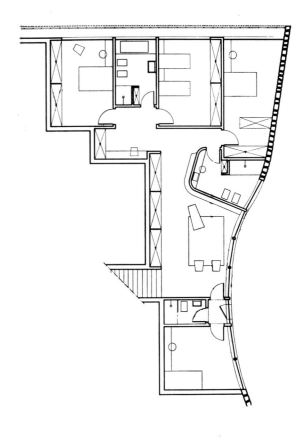

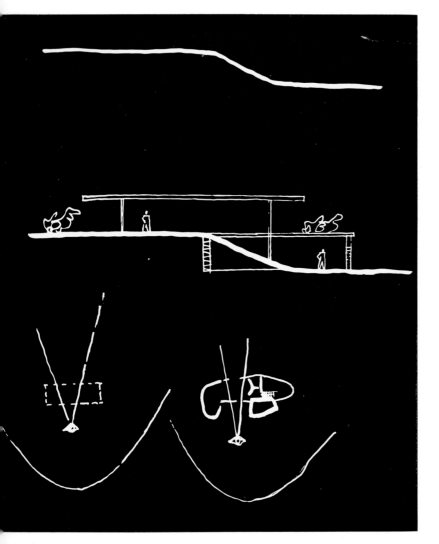

The only attempt at organization is apparent at the lower half-floor (plan above) where four bed rooms, three bath rooms, a small pantry and a space for sitting are provided together with the usual storage for clothes, linen, etc. The core of the plan (sketches on the left and main floor plan on opposite page) is a continuous view on a sloping terrain and a boulder which was retained and offers the only visual obstruction. The kitchen and a water closet are the only enclosed spaces, the rest of the building remaining almost transparent. The canopy, indicated by dotted lines, bears a closer relationship to the shape of the surrounding natural forms than to the floor plan which it shelters.

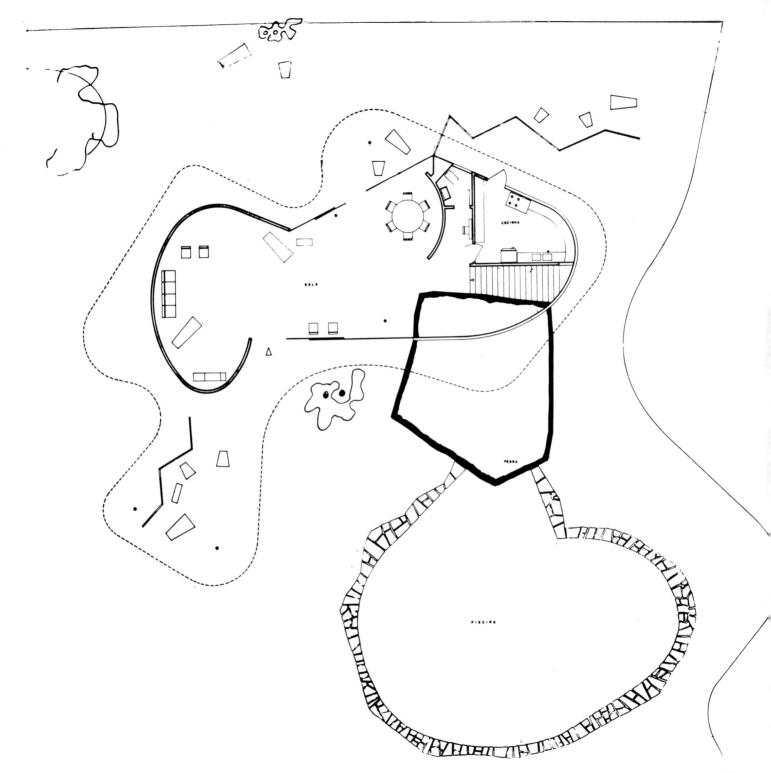

SALA

COZINHA

PEDRA

PISCINA

71

Views of the house seen from the left and the right side of the boulder with some of the movable and permanent screens and the almost uninterrupted wild flora. The role of the statuary, hardly opposing the bulk of the boulder, is, perhaps, to remind one that this is a man-made place.

73

The indoor-outdoor lounging areas are intermittently screened off for visual rest. The picture, above right, shows the dining corner with the kitchen enclosure beyond, the head of the stairs between boulder and kitchen, and the depthless mural formed by the rising hill at the far end. On opposite page: part of the boulder is well within the enclosed area, a kind of interior fixture. A small telescope placed on the top is for those who are interested in details.

On the right and on the opposite page are rear views of the house, the part above the sleeping quarters (see section on page 70). A protective railing encloses the children's terrace. The picture below shows the path, which is the main access to the house, beyond the pond and the statuary.

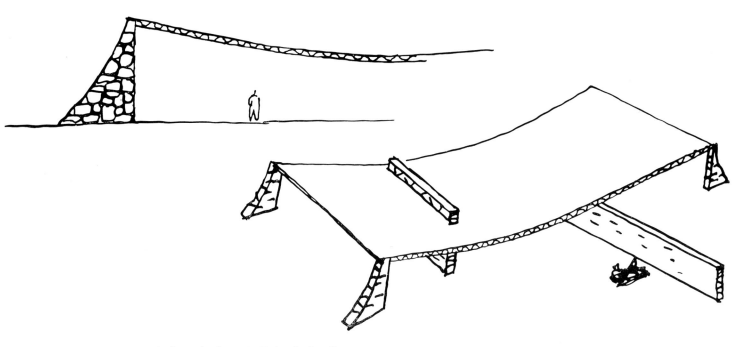

1954. Cavanelas house in Pedro do Rio. Structural Engineer: Amrein. A roof hung from four corner piers of field stone povides a simple shelter for country living. Some masonry screens and occasional statuary interrupt the space under and around this tentlike structure. Three bed rooms, bath, kitchen and living room occupy but a fragment of the total covered space. The impression given is of a completely open structure, like a park pavilion, offering a minimum interference with the surrounding landscape.

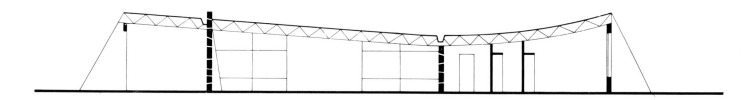

Below is a picture showing the structural elements, the four stone piers, the light steel beams acting as ropes and the nonsupporting screens of masonry. On the opposite page is the finished building and the plan with its simple, straightforward organization; 1, living room; 2, bed rooms; 3, 4, bath room and water closet; 5, kitchen; 6, car port; 7, terrace.

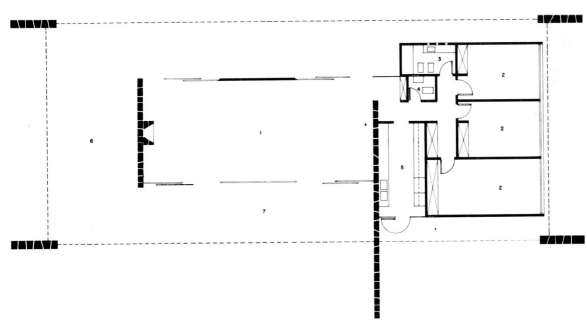

1955. Final project for the Modern Art Museum of Caracas, Venezuela. The finite shape of this structure is in direct contrast with the idea of a "growing museum" proposed by Le Corbusier in 1938. But the role of a Modern Art

Museum is not to provide safekeeping for the general *brouhaha* of an epoch but to maintain a close contact between the public and the artist who labors with the intangibles of his time. "Our desire," says the designer, "was to develop a compact form detaching itself clear- ly from the landscape and expressing in the purity of its lines the forces of contemporary art," and, "to offer to the visitor the surprise and the emotion resulting from a violent con- trast between a sealed exterior and an interior flooded with daylight."

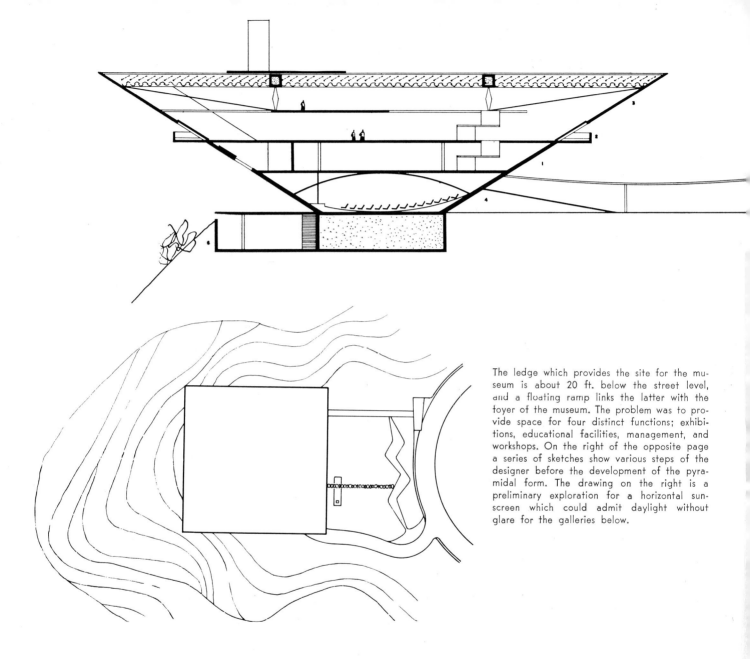

The ledge which provides the site for the museum is about 20 ft. below the street level, and a floating ramp links the latter with the foyer of the museum. The problem was to provide space for four distinct functions; exhibitions, educational facilities, management, and workshops. On the right of the opposite page a series of sketches show various steps of the designer before the development of the pyramidal form. The drawing on the right is a preliminary exploration for a horizontal sunscreen which could admit daylight without glare for the galleries below.

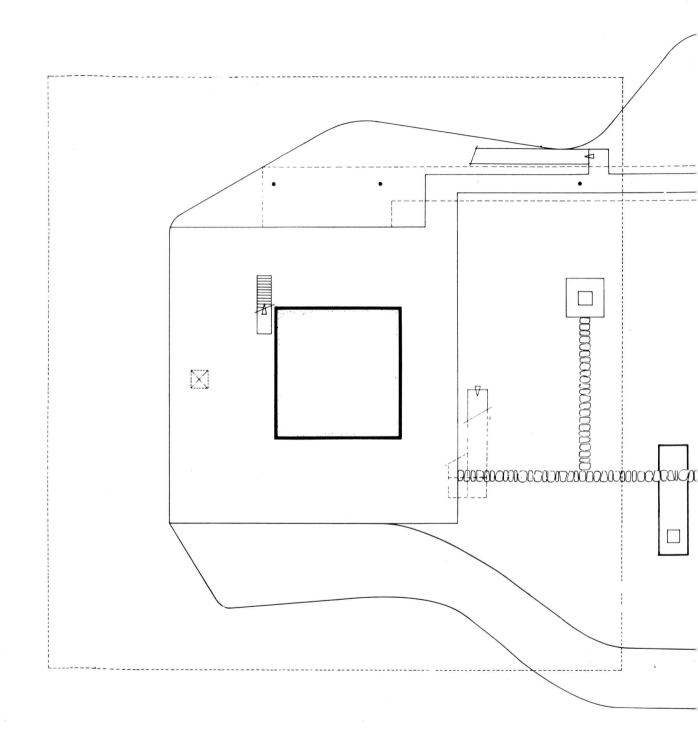

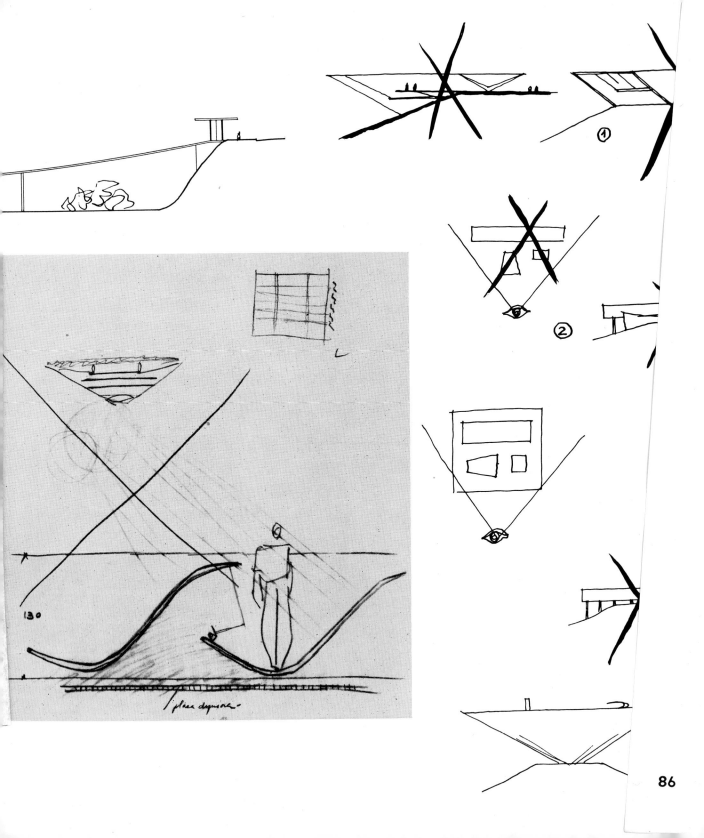

① ② ③

130

place degrace.

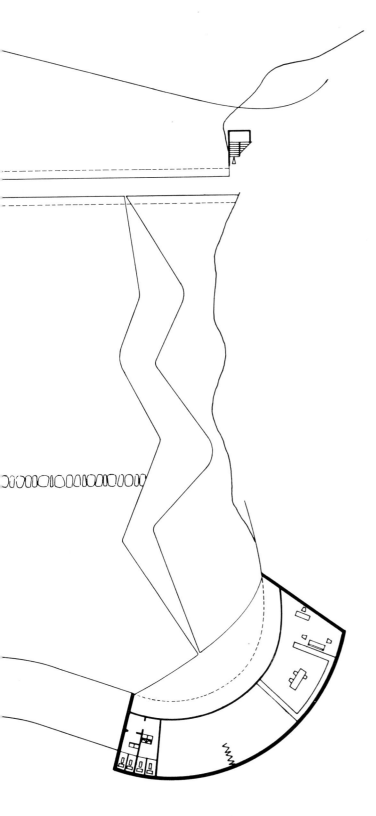

Left: plan at the ground level showing the general layout with stairs (top right) for the art school; a covered passage leading to the school (bottom right); a sculpture garden with a pool and paths of flagstones; a ramp (top) leading to the foyer and another ramp, indicated by dotted lines, leading to the auditorium. The art school consists of two semi separate workshops, a library and an office. Below: partial basement with loading facilities provides space for museum workshops and storage.

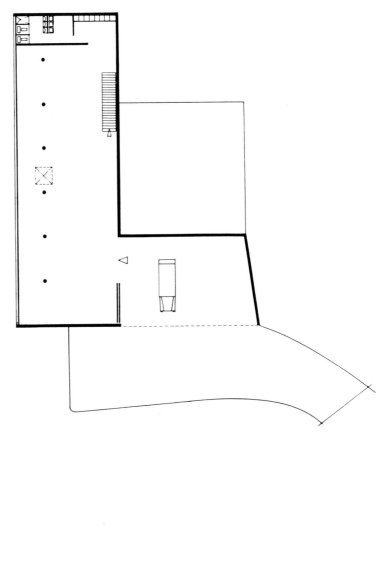

Below: plan of the foyer level with information desk and offices; a ramp on the right leads to the main gallery above. On opposite page: a sketch of the expansive area of the foyer and a plan of the auditorium which has a capacity of 400 seats. The auditorium is located immediately below the foyer and is accessible from the sculpture garden.

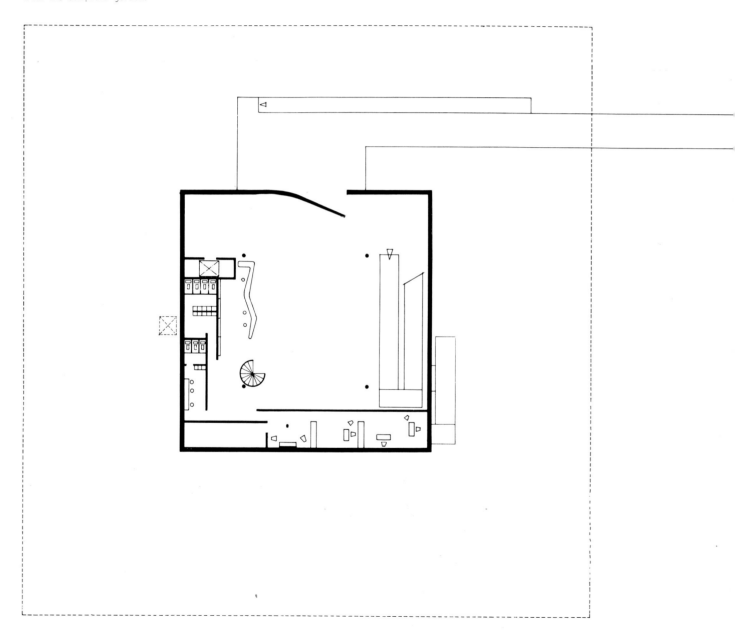

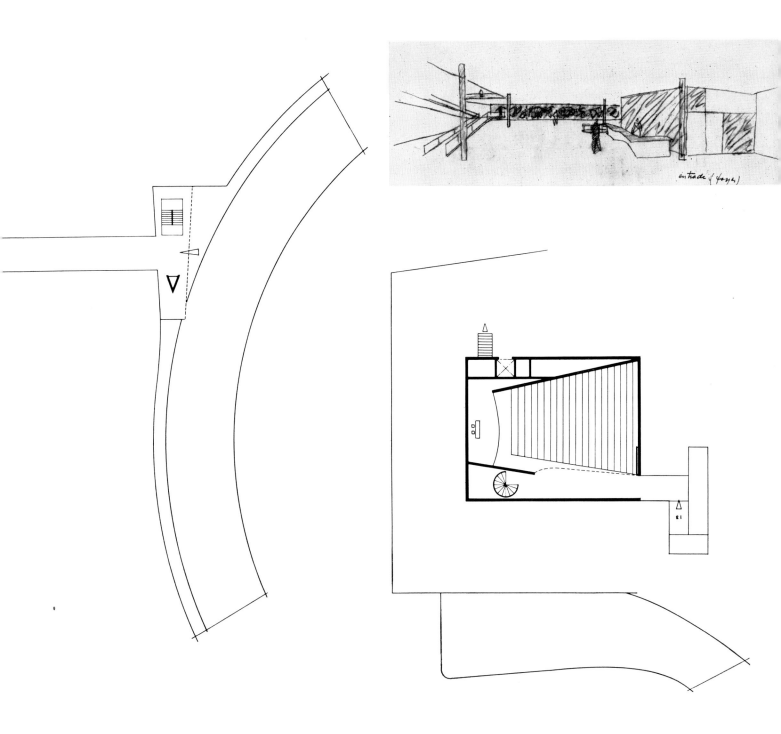

entrée (foyer)

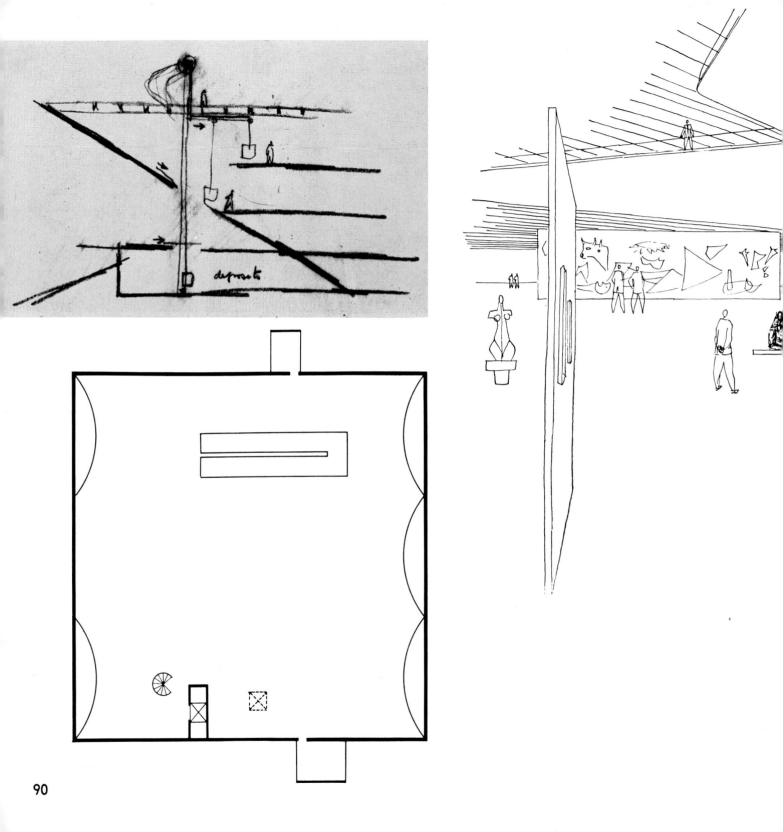

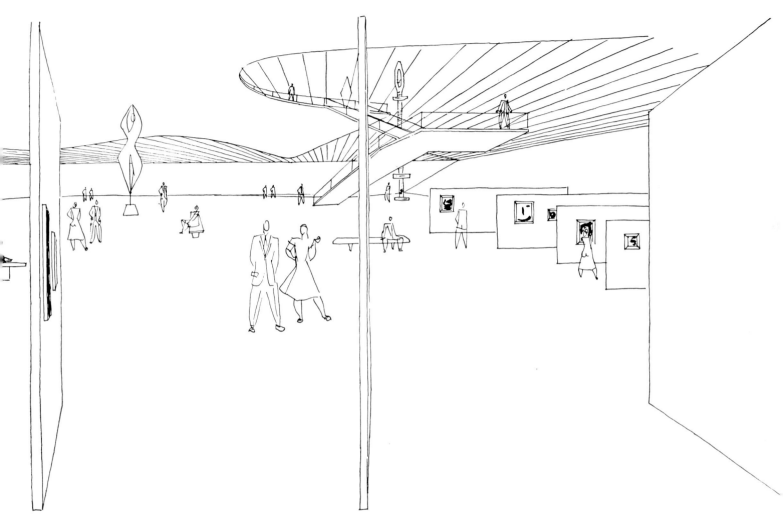

The main gallery with an area of 17,200 sq. ft. is free of any structural elements and permits any arrangement of space and channeling of circulation; it receives controlled daylight from an overhead area of 4,100 sq. ft. due to the fact that the mezzanine above occupies but a fragment of the total area. The sketch on the opposite page shows the device for lifting loads from the storage space in the basement to the galleries and to the roof; its location is indicated on all plans as a small square in dotted lines.

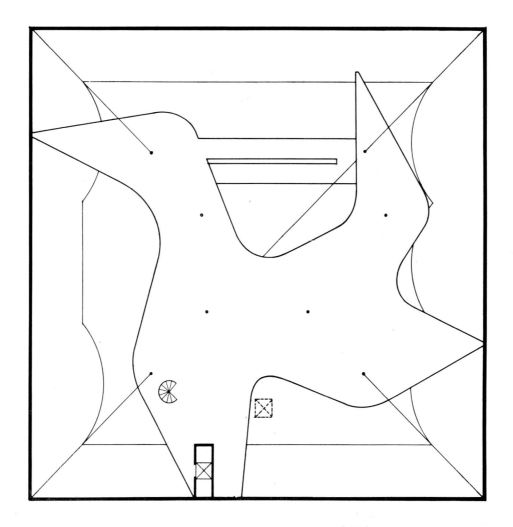

Above: plan of the mezzanine with an exhibition area of 13,100 sq. ft. On opposite page: plan of the roof with an exhibition area of 6,450 sq. ft. The major area of the roof is used to provide daylight for the galleries below. The floor of the mezzanine is suspended from the roof, thus freeing the main gallery from structural supports; a ramp connects the main gallery and the mezzanine.

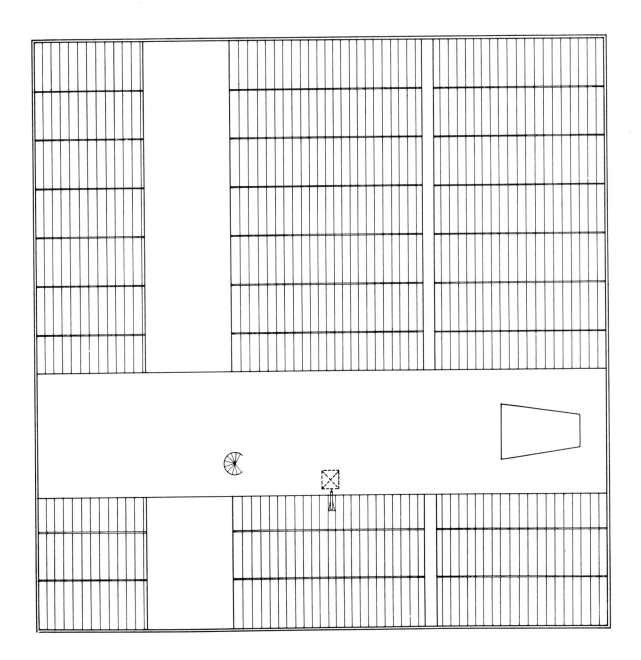

Sketch below: the mezzanine floor is hung from the roof by four rhomboid elements, three of which are shown here. The luminous ceiling (roof) reaches at that level an area of 38,750 ft.; reinforced concrete louvers on the outside and aluminum louvers, carrying fixtures for artificial lighting on the inside, will assure a desirable, controllable light at all times without sharp transitions. Right: plan and sketch of the roof with the paved area for exhibition of sculpture and for public relaxation. At the time the scheme for the museum was established, Alexander Calder was having an exhibition in Caracas; this, perhaps, explains the "mobiles" which appear in both sketches.

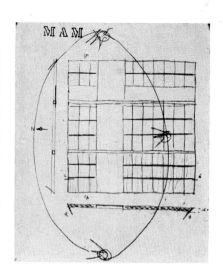

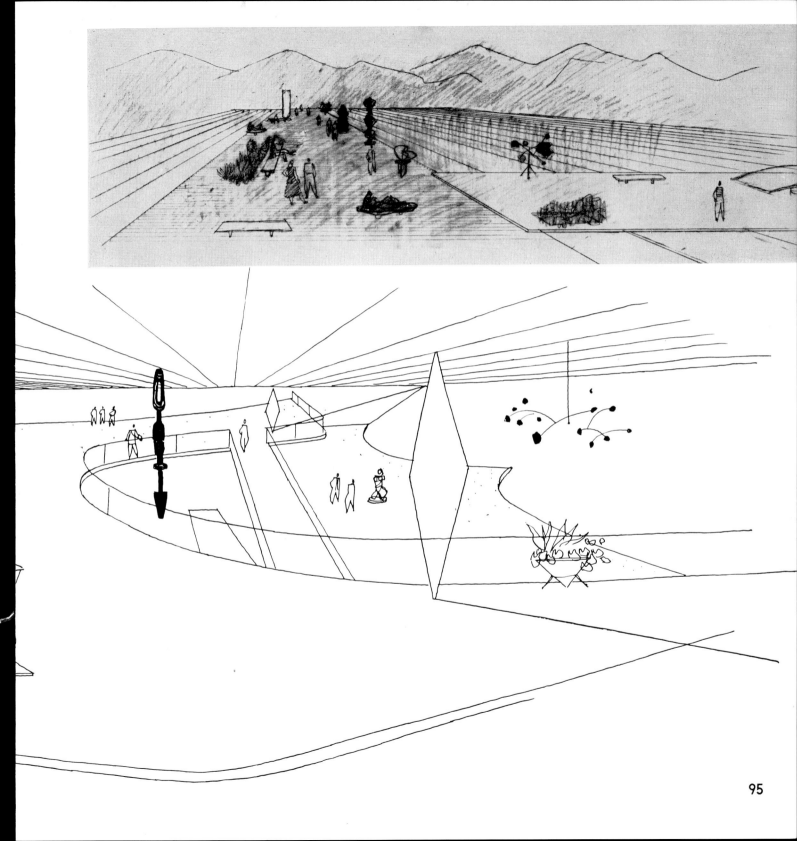

Because of the basic scheme which shapes the building, the façades are of extreme simplicity; it is difficult for one to conceive a building delineated with fewer lines. Top right: south-east façade showing the stairs to the art school and sculpture garden, and the main entrance to the foyer of the museum at the end of the floating ramp. Below: north-west façade with the vehicular ramp leading to the storage space. On opposite page: south-west façade showing the entrance to the auditorium, and, bottom of this page, north-east façade overlooking the down slope.

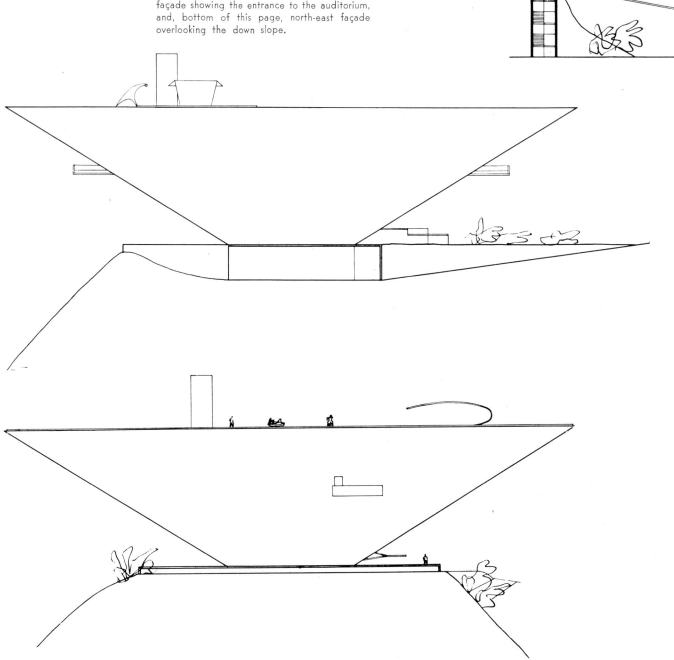

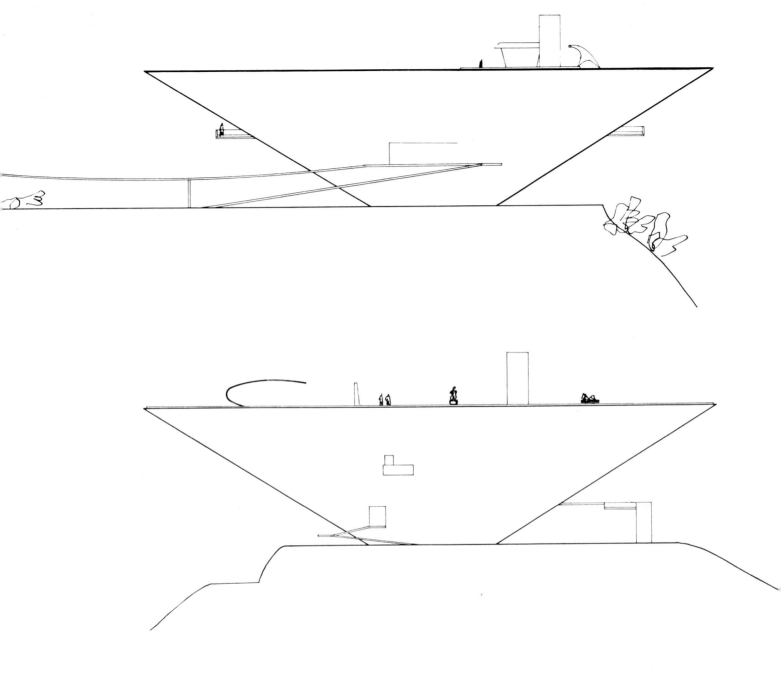

Right: model of the building with the roof omitted in order to show the mezzanine and the main gallery floor below. All floors will be designed to act as ties (with the exception of the mezzanine which is suspended from the roof) thus forcing the weight to be directed towards the base of the inverted pyramid. Each exterior wall will consist of two reinforced concrete slabs, each one 2⅝ in. thick with ribs 2 ft. 6 in. deep and 3 ft. 3⅜ in. (1 meter) off center. Electric outlets on the exhibition floors will provide additional, localized lighting.

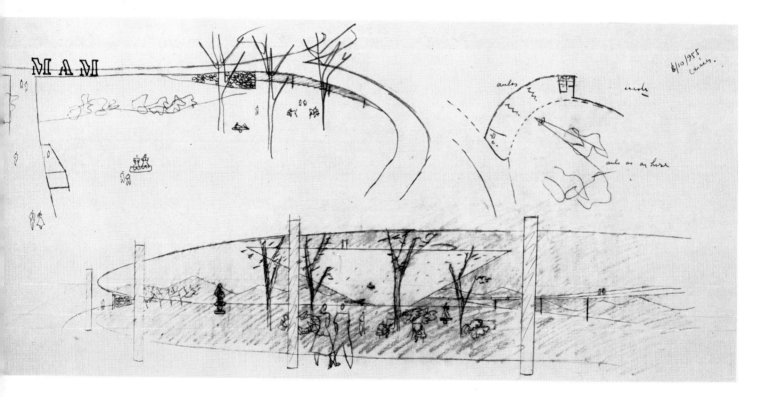

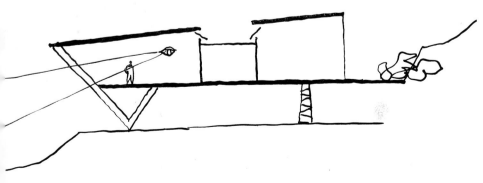

1951. Hotel at Diamantina. Structural Engineer: Joaquim Cardozo. Photography: M. Gautherot. This and the following three buildings, a school, an air depot and a social club, are located in a small town with a population of a little over 10,000, north-east of Belo Horizonte, in the state of Minas Gerais. Built on sloping terrain overlooking the town, this small hotel consists of a ground floor, with public terraces and halls, and a second floor with guest rooms. The latter enjoy cross-ventilation because of the lower ceiling of the center corridor. The stilts here are designed to support not only the floor above but also the overhang of the roof which shields the front rooms; each span is slightly over 20 ft.

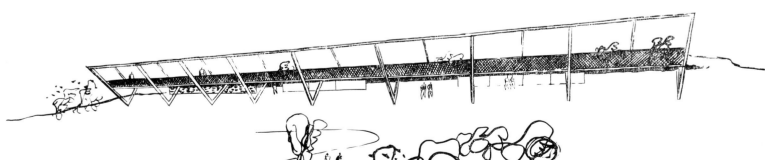

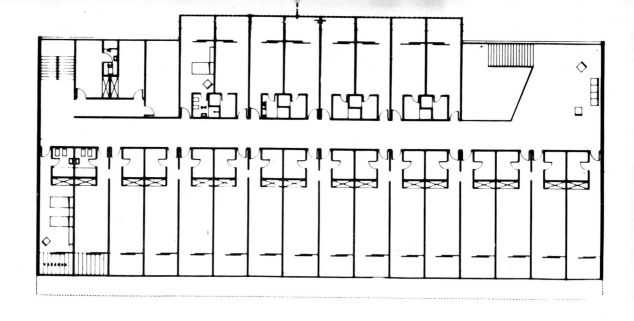

Below: ground floor plan, showing the main hall and reception desk at upper right, a restaurant in the center, kitchen and service stairs on the left. Above: 2nd floor plan with 24 guest rooms, each one with terrace and bath room, and one apartment (upper left).

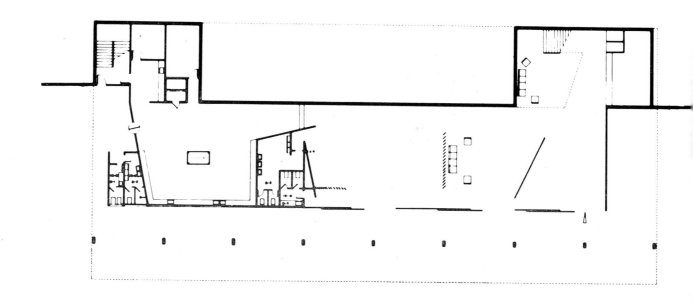

1951. Julia Kubitscheck School at Diamantina. Structural Engineer: W. Muller. Photography: M. Gautherot. Planned as a grammar school and situated also on a sloping terrain like the hotel Diamantina, this building shows a structural variation—the stilts are of an oval section, and separate brackets from the 2nd floor support the overhanging roof, which protects the class rooms.

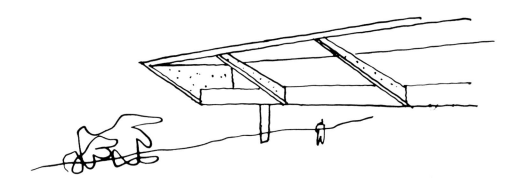

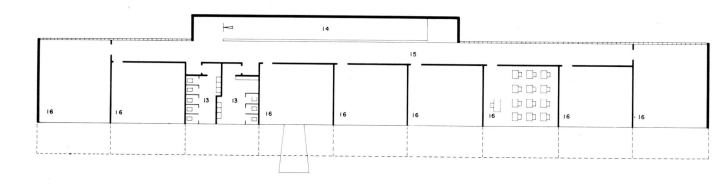

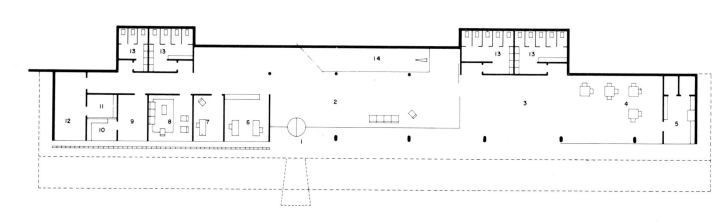

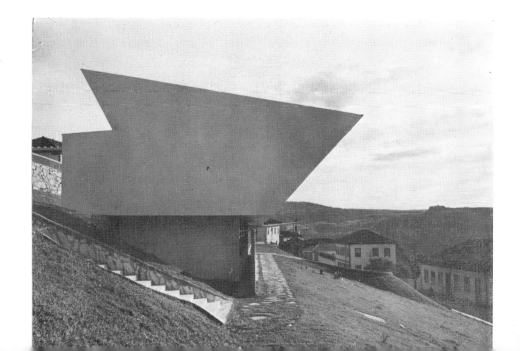

Ground floor plan (opposite page, center): 1, 2, entrance and hall; 3, terrace; 4, refectory; 5, kitchen; 6-8, secretary, principal and teachers' rooms; 9, 10, dental and medical dispensary; 14, ramp. The 2nd floor contains 8 class rooms, all on one side of the corridor. Right: section shows that cross-ventilation and additional daylight are secured over the roof of the ramp and the corridor.

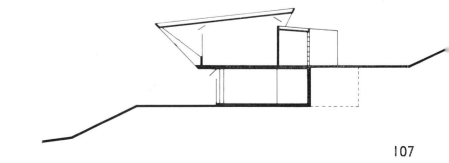

On opposite page: views of the ground floor, showing the screen in front of the kitchen and the sheltered area which is to be used during recess in inclement weather. On this page: views of the ramp seen from the ground floor (left) and from the upper floor (above).

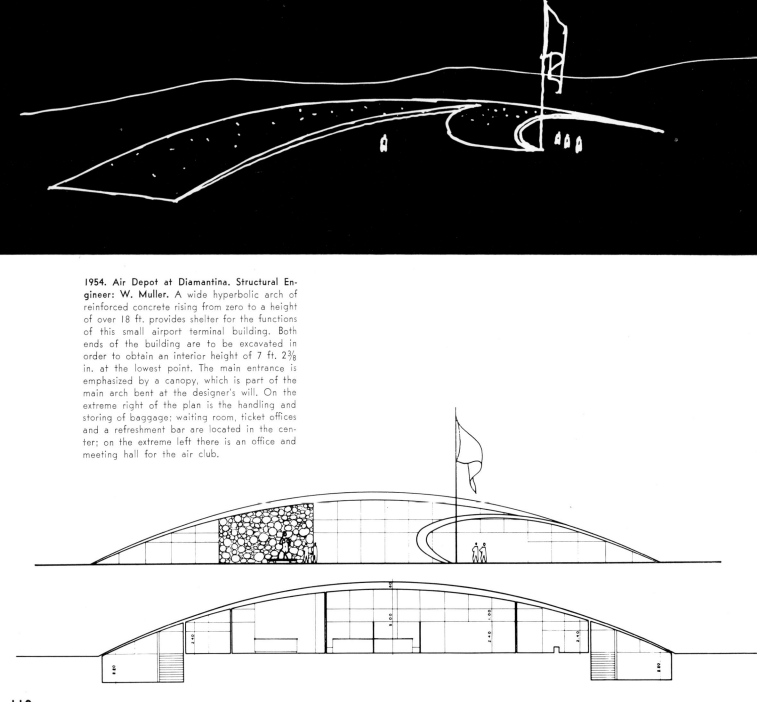

1954. Air Depot at Diamantina. Structural Engineer: W. Muller. A wide hyperbolic arch of reinforced concrete rising from zero to a height of over 18 ft. provides shelter for the functions of this small airport terminal building. Both ends of the building are to be excavated in order to obtain an interior height of 7 ft. 2⅜ in. at the lowest point. The main entrance is emphasized by a canopy, which is part of the main arch bent at the designer's will. On the extreme right of the plan is the handling and storing of baggage; waiting room, ticket offices and a refreshment bar are located in the center; on the extreme left there is an office and meeting hall for the air club.

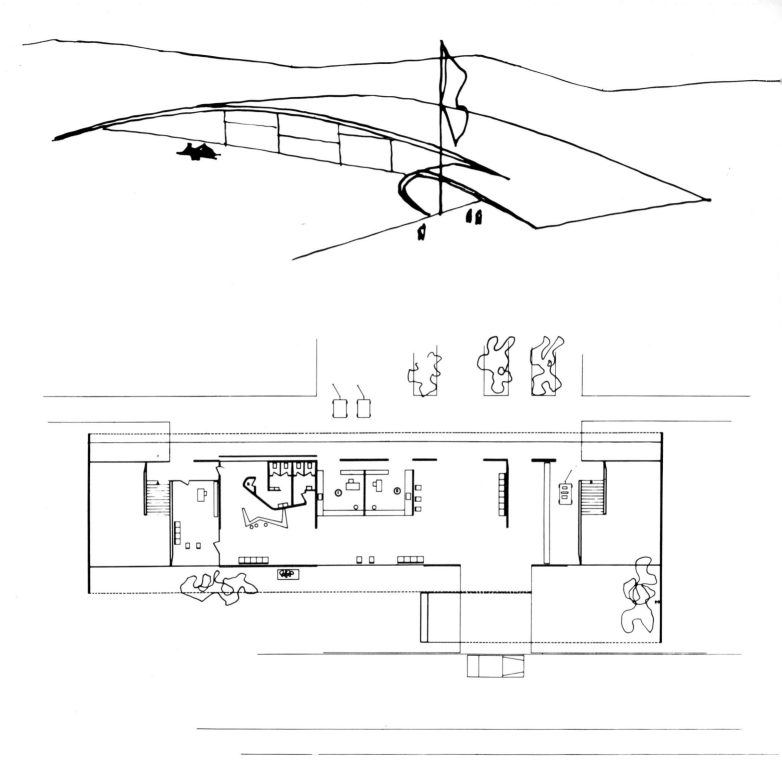

1950. Club at Diamantina. Structural Engineer: W. Muller. Photography: R. Landau. A raised platform and an independent hyperbolic arch, forming the roof, are the structural elements of this building. Part of the ground is left open so as not to obstruct the view for the members entering from the higher side of a gentle slope (section on opposite page). It is for the same reason that kitchen and services are located below in a semibasement. The picture on top of this page shows the entrance to the club with a self-standing, cantilevered canopy.

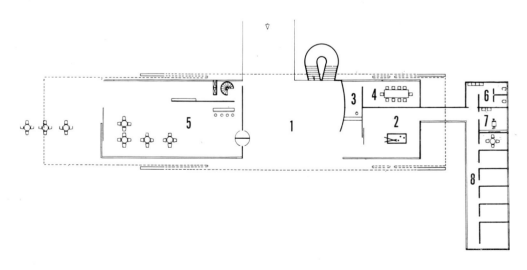

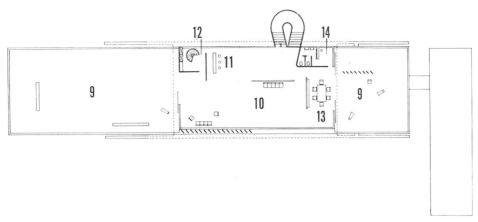

Ground floor plan (opposite page): 1, entrance; 2, game room; 3, desk; 4, private dining room; 5, restaurant; 6, rest rooms; 7, barbershop; 8, private game rooms. Second floor plan (above): 9, roof garden; 10, lounge; 11, bar; 12, service; 13, reading room. The extensive gardens surrounding the club include a music shed and a swimming pool, both located at the rear of the building (picture below).

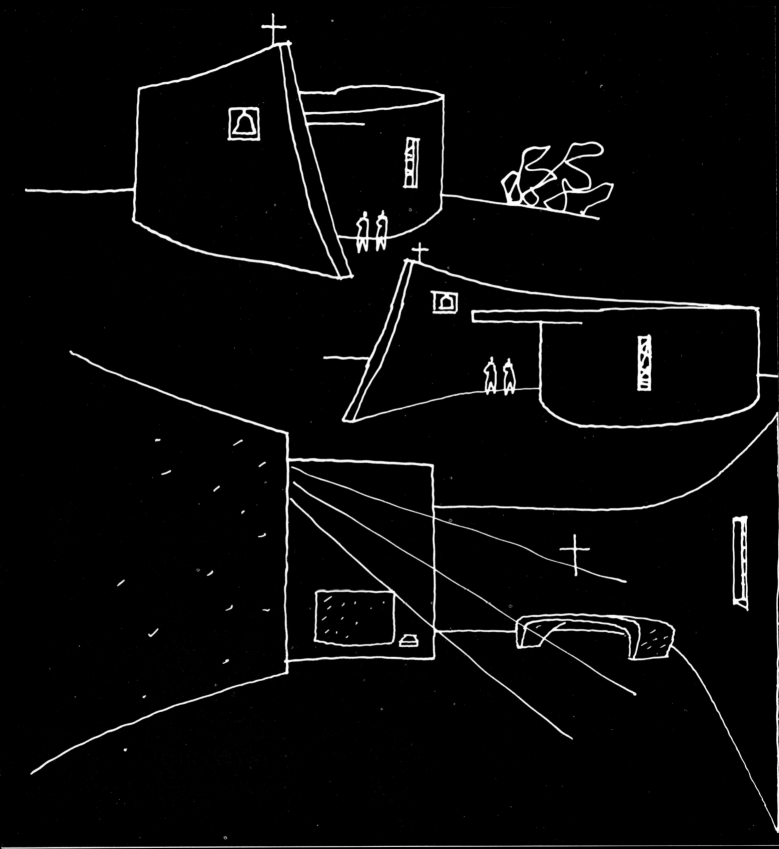

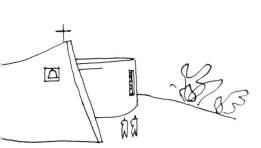

1955. Project for a chapel. This humble building with a paraphrased nautilus plan has a pulpit, two high steps above the ground and cantilevered from the wall which partitions the sacristy, and an altar well lighted from the major source of daylight. A hole in the wall, which forms an off center narthex, provides a place for the bell. In spite of the simplicity of the plan, those who enter, because of the direction from which they must enter, will have a momentary impression of stepping into a crypt or a labyrinth.

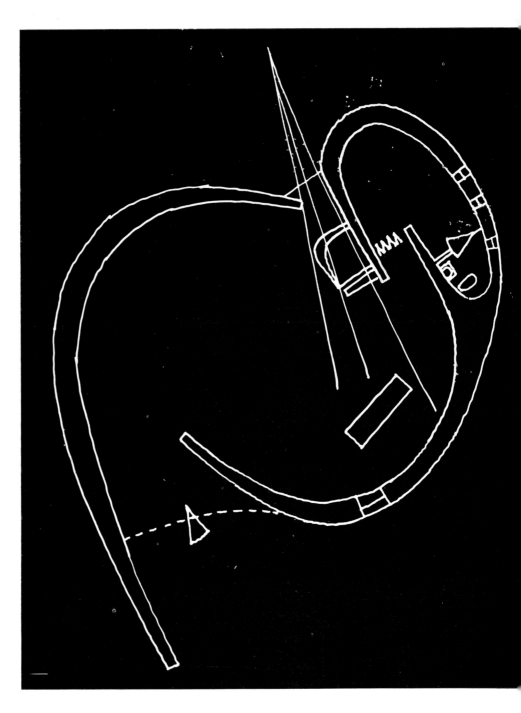

1952. Automobile service station at São Paolo.
Five barrel-vaults supported at their springings
by reinforced concrete partitions form an overhead protection for 2, a waiting room; 4,
offices; 3, rest rooms; and 5, storage—all shown
in plan on opposite page. A perforated curtain
wall located well within the building line allows a generous overhanging of the vaultings
and helps the building retain the clarity of
its structural lines. This curtain wall was partially erected at the time the picture above
was taken. A flat canopy, in contrast with the
barrel-vaults, shelters the gasoline pumps and
the lubrication pits (6 and 7 on the plan); it
is held by supports, the design of which is both
structural and sculptural.

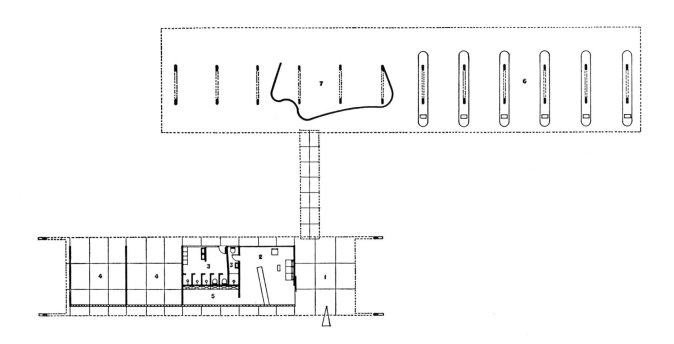

On opposite page: side elevation showing a low covered passage linking the pumps' shelter with the portico of the main building, a simple, post and lintel structure. Right: the boomeranglike pylon situated near the traffic road has the dual role of being a support and a visual attraction. It can be clearly seen from the picture on opposite page—and it is gratifying—that the structural supports overpower the shapes of the packaged pumps and of the inflated vehicles; reduced to a toylike scale they both remain unrelated to anything else.

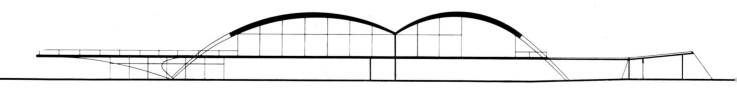

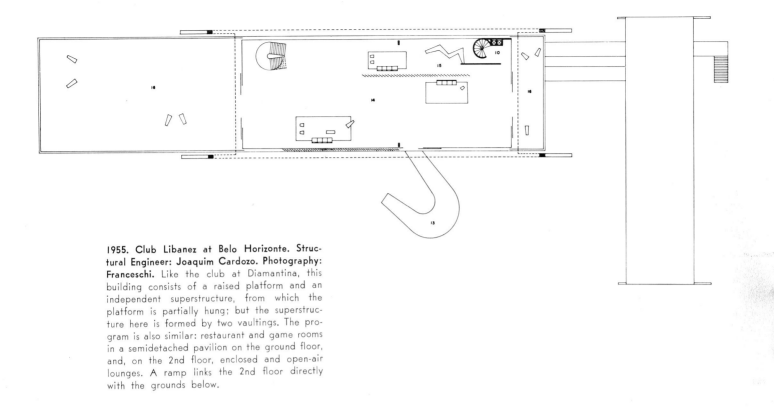

1955. Club Libanez at Belo Horizonte. Structural Engineer: Joaquim Cardozo. Photography: Franceschi. Like the club at Diamantina, this building consists of a raised platform and an independent superstructure, from which the platform is partially hung; but the superstructure here is formed by two vaultings. The program is also similar: restaurant and game rooms in a semidetached pavilion on the ground floor, and, on the 2nd floor, enclosed and open-air lounges. A ramp links the 2nd floor directly with the grounds below.

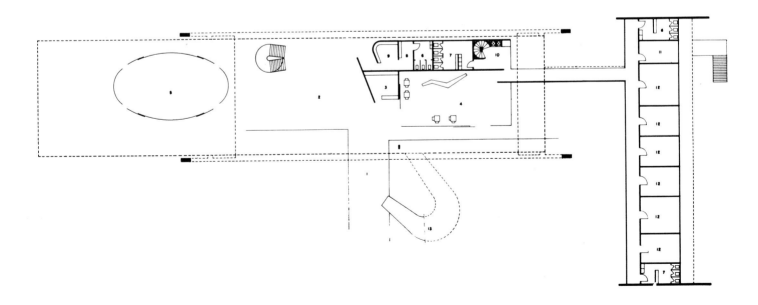

1951. IV Centenary Exhibition of São Paolo. Associate Architects: Helio Uchoa, Zenon Lotufo, Eduardo Kneese de Mello. Collaborators: Gauss Estelita, Carlos Lemos. Structural Engineer: Joaquim Cardozo. Photography: Franceschi. Built to commemorate the four-hundredth anniversary, which took place in 1954, of the founding of the city of São Paolo, this exhibition, unlike others, is of a permanent character. Buildings and park, at the end of the fair, will become additional educational and recreational facilities for the citizens of São Paolo. The aerial view on the opposite page shows the fair grounds and the buildings in the center near the artificial lakes and, in the foreground, the construction of a new sports center for the city, an independent but concurrent activity. The architect of the sports center is Icaro de Castro Mello.

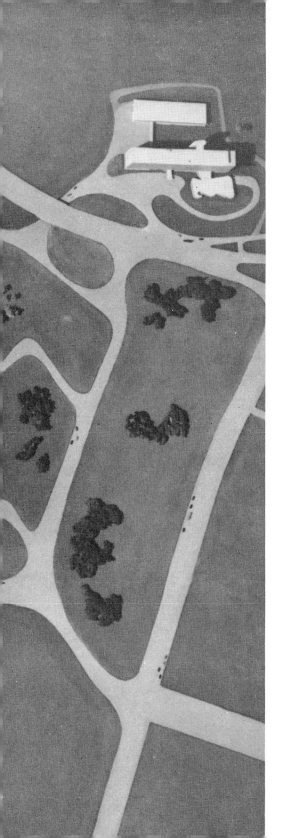

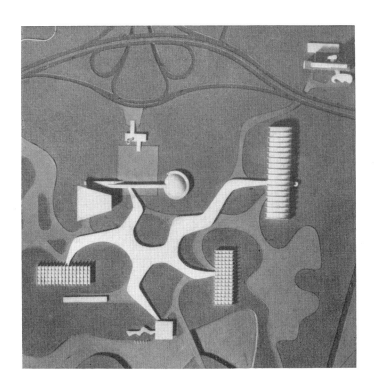

With the exception, perhaps, of the Stockholm Exhibition of 1930, under the direct responsibility of the late Asplund, no other similar undertaking has been conceived as a single project and carried out by such an homogenous group of designers. Buildings here are not like wayside flowers among many weeds, located on conveniently prescribed lots, and the public is not left to itself, and at its risk, to assort and prepare a balance sheet of its emotional impact in streets and avenues of side shows. Above: the original plan with its main feature, the octopus like canopy, 2,000 ft. long, which links all the main buildings (clockwise): a spherical structure for art exhibits, the Hall of Industry, the Hall of Nations, a restaurant by the lake, the Hall of States and an auditorium with 2,000 seats. The Avenue Nova Anhangabau (top) and the Avenue of Brazil (left-right) provide, at their intersection, the main access to the exhibition grounds; a small raised entrance pavilion (left off center) allows the visitor to grasp the fair as a whole. A square, formal esplanade is in front of the entrance pavilion between the Auditorium and the Arts Build-ing; the canopy starts near the end of the esplanade and provides a sinuous covered access to the various points of interest. At the upper right corner, not linked by the canopy, is the Hall of Agriculture, which is planned to house some permanent services of the Ministry. An artificial narrow lake, at the left and bottom of the plan, and a number of meandering paths complete the pattern of what will be, at the end of the fair, the Ibirapuera Park. Left: the plan as it has been approved by the fair commission—"mutilated" according to the expression of the designers. A number of minor, but, perhaps, decisive changes are noticeable, all made in the name of economy and expediency. The entrance pavilion is eliminated and the public enters directly into the esplanade; the shape of the canopy is considerably simplified and the total length reduced by locating the Hall of Nations near the Hall of States and by omitting the link with the restaurant. The circulation pattern becomes a flat inverted T. Also, for reasons of expediency, the structural design of three major buildings is simplified, as can be noticed in the approved model.

127

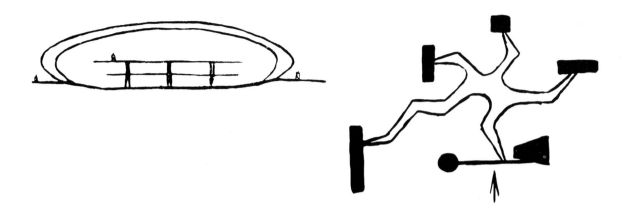

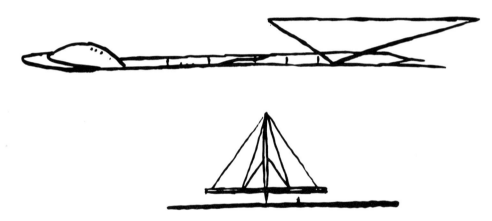

On opposite page: detail views of the final model taken from the access avenues (top) and from the lake at the rear (bottom). Above: a sketch of the original structural concept for three large buildings: the Halls of Nations, of States and of Industry. An independent shell covers a free standing, multistory structure; this was superseded by a more conventional method of construction. Sketches on the right: initial proposals (top to bottom) for the canopy, the Arts Pavilion and Auditorium, the restaurant with a roof suspended from a center mast, and a structural sculpture.

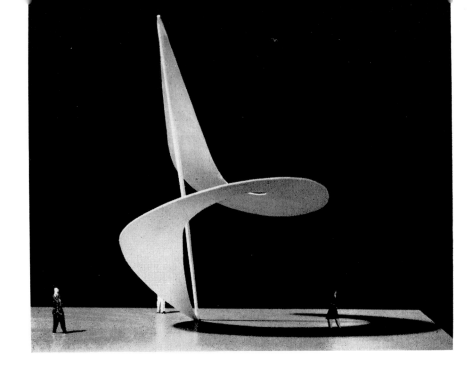

The thematic structure, a model of which is shown here, was originally conceived for the entrance pavilion; its symbolism is clear enough to remind every visitor that São Paolo is "the fastest growing city of the world." Modest in its dimensions if not in its virtual movement, this structural sculpture consists of a reinforced concrete pole with deep foundations and of a steel framed and metal clad helicoidal plane in an ascending position; the latter counter-balances the slanting angle of the pole. The total height is 39 ft. 4$\frac{3}{8}$ in. (12 meters) with a maximum width of 16 ft. 4$\frac{3}{4}$ in. (5 meters). Preliminary structural studies were made by the engineer Jose Carlos Figueiredo Ferraz. The omission of the entrance pavilion from the original scheme resulted in the final elimination of this structure.

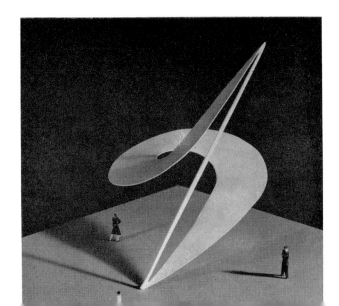

On this page: views of the canopy, one taken from the air and the other at pedestrian level. The V-shaped supports replace the columns in the proximity of each building, thus allowing a large portion of the canopy to be cantilevered and freeing the accesses to the buildings. On opposite page: the Hall of Nations is shown at bottom left and, on its right, the Hall of States; directly opposite to this group of buildings is the Hall of Industry. Beyond, across the tree-lined Avenue of Brazil, is the Hall of Agriculture, linked with an underpass to the fair grounds.

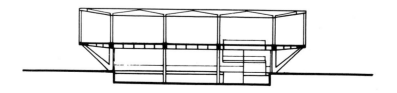

Hall of States. Above: the picture of the model shows the Hall of States, on the top, and the Hall of Nations on the right; both buildings are identical as to plans and sections but have different façade treatments because of the difference in orientation. The Hall of States provides exhibition area for the twenty Brazilian states on two levels, ground and 2nd floor. On opposite page: the main façade has a northeast orientation and a honeycomb type of sunscreen. Right: the rear façade has vertical adjustable louvers. Below: the main approach to the building under the canopy.

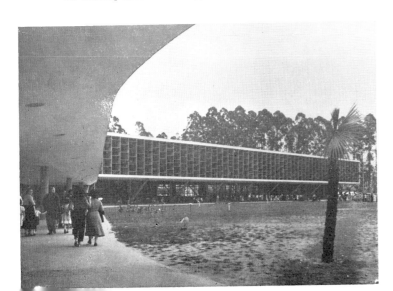

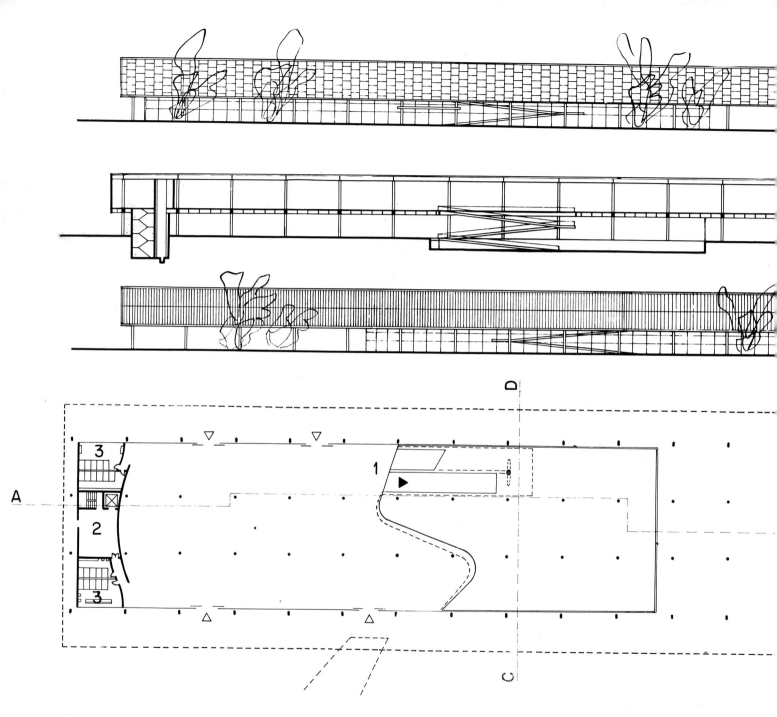

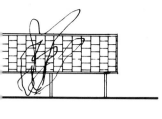

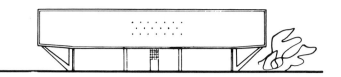

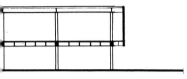

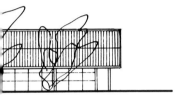

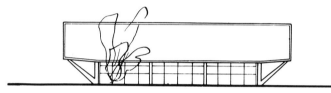

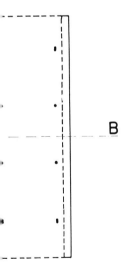

B

From top to bottom: main elevation (north-east) and lateral elevation (south-east); longitudinal section on A-B axis showing the depressed part of the ground floor and the development of the ramp; rear elevation (south-west) with vertical louvers and north-west elevation. Dotted lines on the ground floor plan indicate the cantilevered 2nd floor and its connection with the canopy; a considerable part of the ground floor is left open to the outdoors. 1, ramp down to the depressed area and up to the second floor; 2, storage; 3, rest rooms.

Details of the honeycomb sunscreen with perforated horizontal louvers. The adopted structural system with free standing columns and bracket supported screen walls is clearly shown in the picture on the opposite page; it is in contrast with the original scheme consisting of an independent shell sheltering a free-standing interior structure (see sketch of the section on page 129). Basement plan (bottom of the page): 1, mechanical equipment; 2, storage; 3, pumps; 4, emergency generator; 5, transformer. Dotted lines indicate the enclosed area of the ground floor. 2nd floor plan (directly below): 1, ramp; 2, storage; 3, rest rooms.

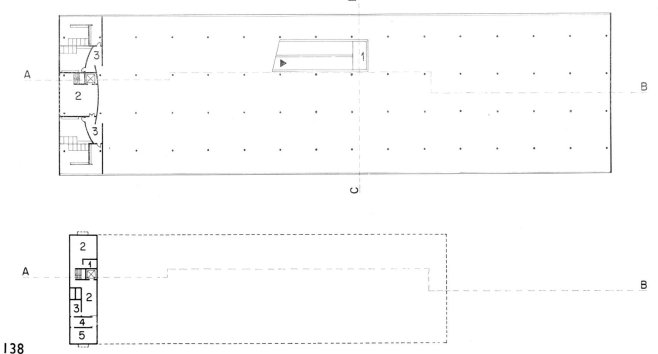

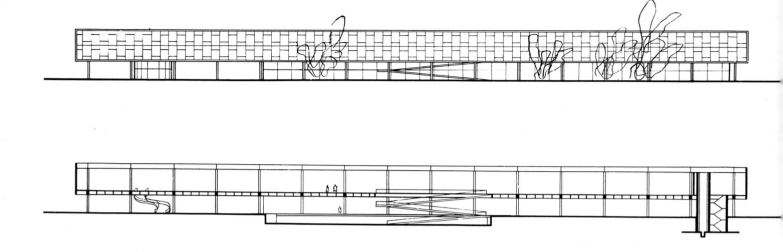

Hall of Nations. Of a similar plan and at a
right angle to the preceding building, the Hall
of Nations provides space for the participation
of other countries in the São Paolo exhibition.
Top of the page: the south-east elevation. Below: view of the same elevation seen from
under the canopy. On opposite page: rear
view of the building.

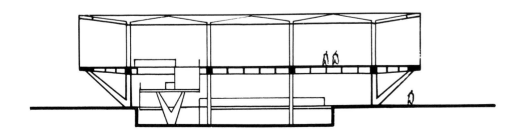

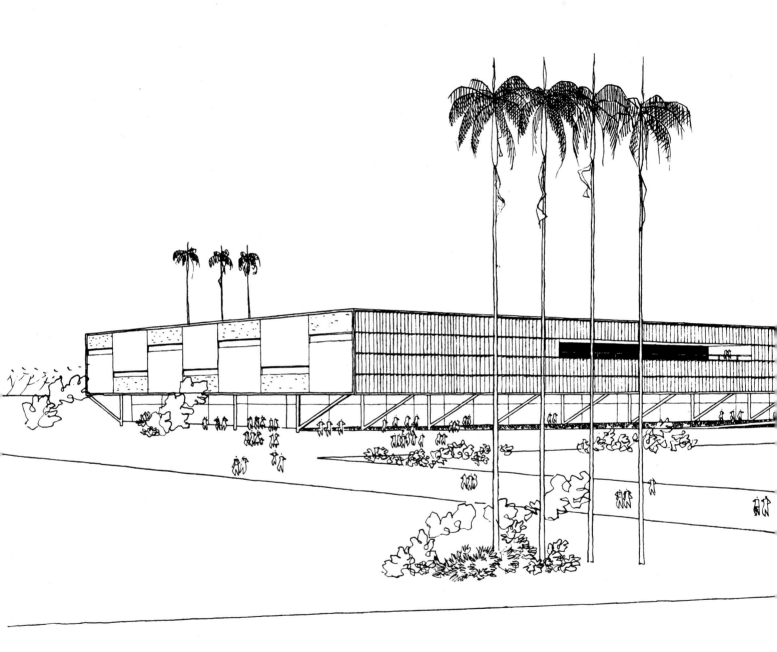

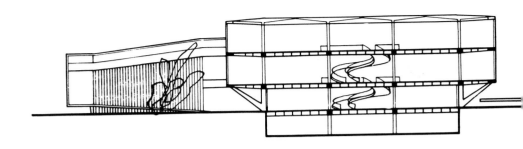

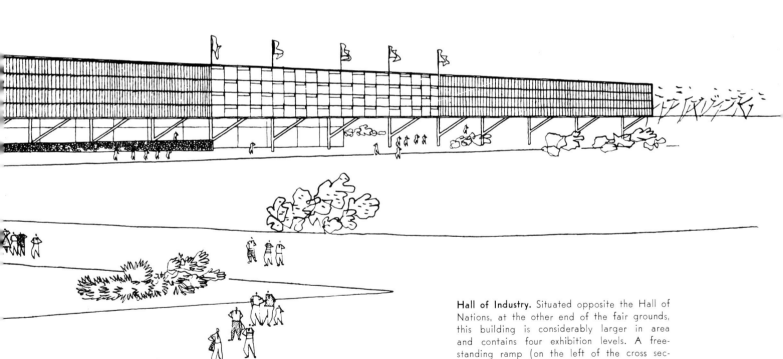

Hall of Industry. Situated opposite the Hall of Nations, at the other end of the fair grounds, this building is considerably larger in area and contains four exhibition levels. A free-standing ramp (on the left of the cross section) provides the main link between levels; another ramp, of a horseshoe shape, and a set of escalators, located in the center of the building, offer additional facilities. Above: perspective shows the main elevation of the building facing north-west, with a similar type of construction as in the preceding Halls: free standing columns and tapering brackets, circular in section, support the overhang of the floor above.

143

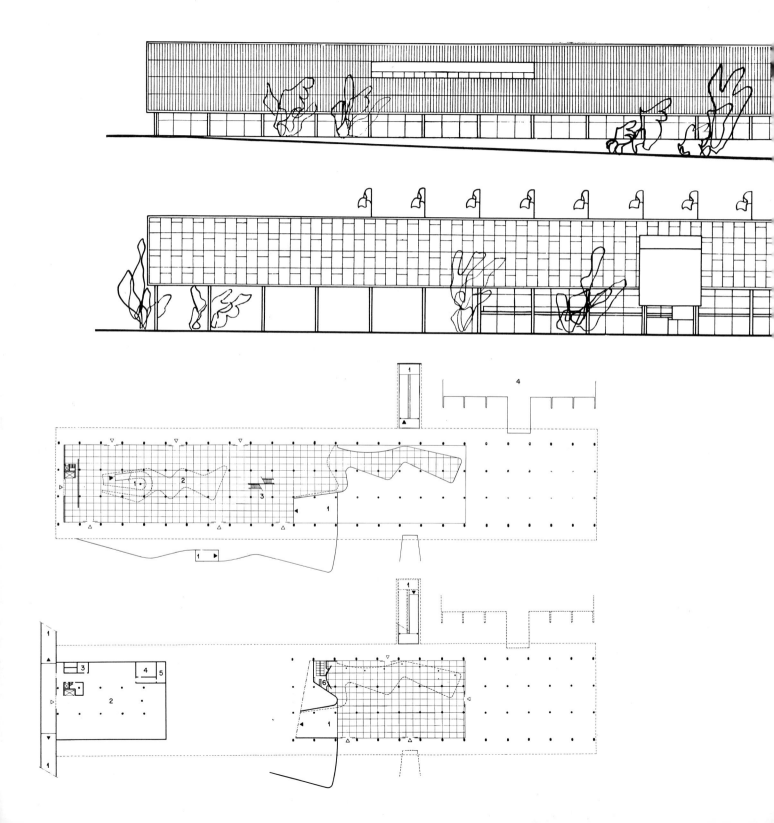

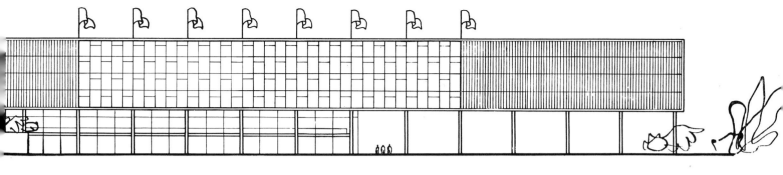

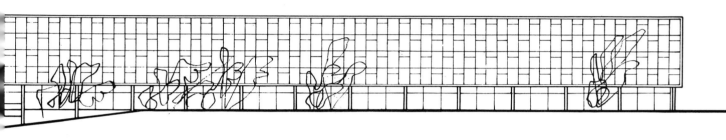

Above: rear elevation (south-east) and main elevation (north-west) on top of the page. Opposite page: plans of the partial basement and of the ground floor show that the enclosed area, indicated with squares, is a fraction of the total area of the building. Right: free standing ramp offers a sculptural element to the building; when in use, the movement of the traffic will provide additional attraction through animation.

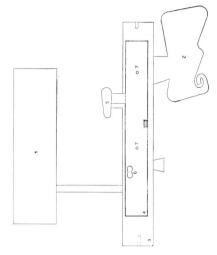

Hall of Agriculture. This multistory building (ground, mezzanine and 8 upper floors) is an annex of the Ministry of Agriculture and it is designed to house permanent services. Situated outside of the main fair grounds, it is connected with them by an underpass. Besides the main building there is a two-story garage, 1, and a semidetached restaurant-pavilion, 2. The stilts transfer the loads carried by two columns to a single point of support on the ground allowing, thus, a considerable freedom for the planning of the ground floor.

147

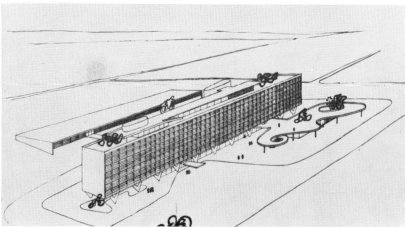

Above: helicoidal stairs leading to the roof of the restaurant and to the mezzanine floor of the main building. Ground floor plan (below): 1, employees' hall; 2, public hall; 3, entrance of high functionaries; 4, passage to the garage; 5, exhibition space; 6, bar; 7, kitchen; 8, restaurant; 9, lounge; 10-14, basement equipment and storage space under the kitchen and the public hall.

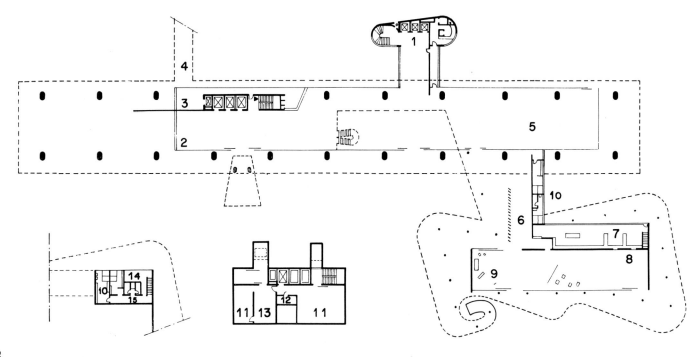

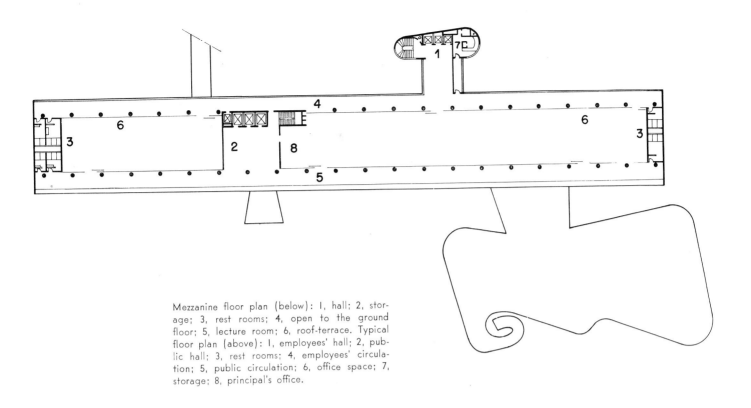

Mezzanine floor plan (below): 1, hall; 2, storage; 3, rest rooms; 4, open to the ground floor; 5, lecture room; 6, roof-terrace. Typical floor plan (above): 1, employees' hall; 2, public hall; 3, rest rooms; 4, employees' circulation; 5, public circulation; 6, office space; 7, storage; 8, principal's office.

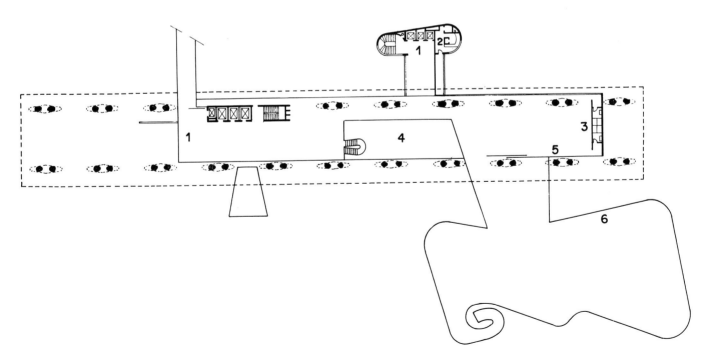

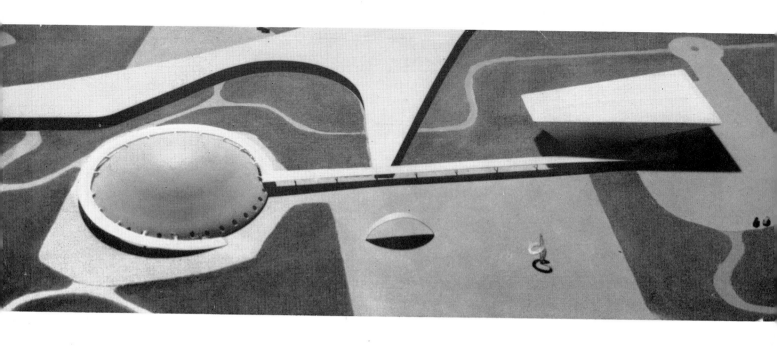

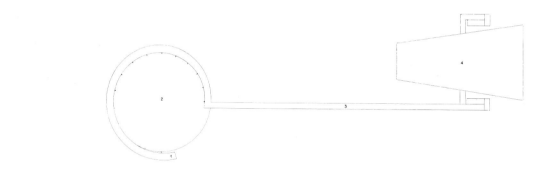

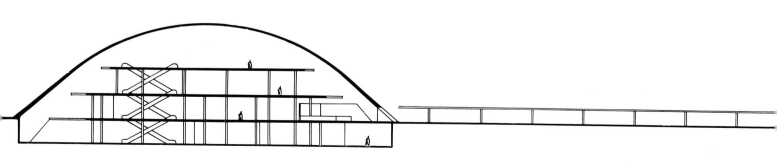

Auditorium and Pavilion of the Arts. A reinforced concrete dome sheltering the Arts Pavilion lies directly on the ground, while the 2,000 seat auditorium has its contact with the ground reduced to a minimum (section at the bottom of the page). A ringlike ramp around the dome, connected with a walk raised above the esplanade, links the two structures. Four tiers of exhibition space, serviced by a set of escalators and a ramp, are under the enclosure of the dome. On the right of the esplanade is the thematic sculpture, and, on the left, an arched structure, the only purpose of which is to present a mural on its intrados. The construction of the Auditorium, the raised walk, the sculpture and the arch was suspended for reasons of economy. Below and right are exterior and interior views of the portholes near the base of the dome, the only source of daylight for the art exhibits.

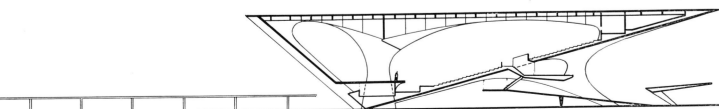

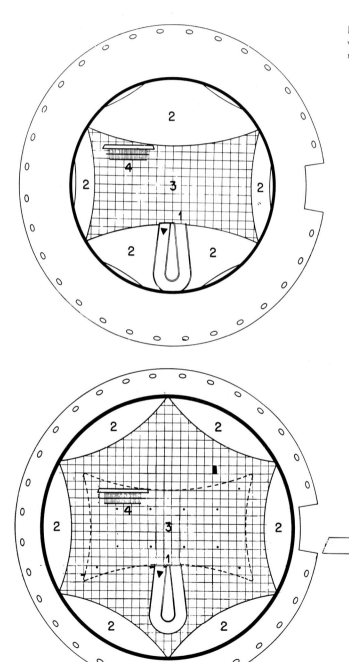

Below: plan of the third level of the Arts Pavilion, and, above it, plan of the top level. 1, ramp; 2, open; 3, exhibition area; 4, escalators.

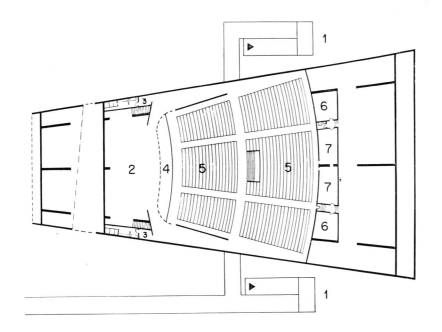

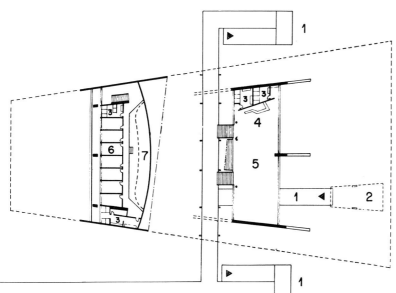

Above: plan of the Auditorium at the foyer level. 1, ramps; 2, marquee; 3, rest rooms; 4, bar; 5, foyer; 6, dressing rooms. On the top of the page is a plan taken on a higher level showing the stage, the seating arrangement and the projection booths. Right: plan at ground level. Indicated in solid black are the very few points of contact which the Auditorium maintains with the ground.

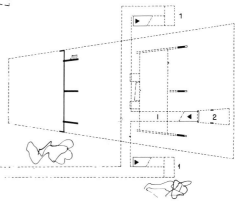

1954. Secondary school building at Belo Horizonte. Structural Engineer: Z. Glabe. Photography: M. Gautherot and Franceschi. The high grounds upon which the school is being built are linked with the street level by a ramp in the form of a loop. Free standing on the grounds is the auditorium; its shape is derived, according to the sketches on opposite page, by inscribing the speaker and the audience in a minimum, useful enclosure. The diagram on the far right shows the four main elements of the plan: 1, classrooms; 2, administration; 3, students' club; 4, auditorium. The classroom wing is 65 ft. 6 in. wide by 345 ft. long, while the length of the auditorium is 125 ft. and its width tapers from 88 ft. 6 in. to 44 ft. 3⅜ in. at the rear of the stage. The span between two stilts corresponds with the length of a classroom, approximately 23 ft. A sculpture-flagpole on the axis of the auditorium dominates the grounds.

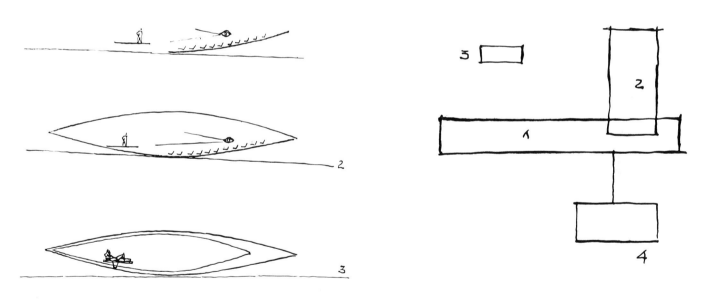

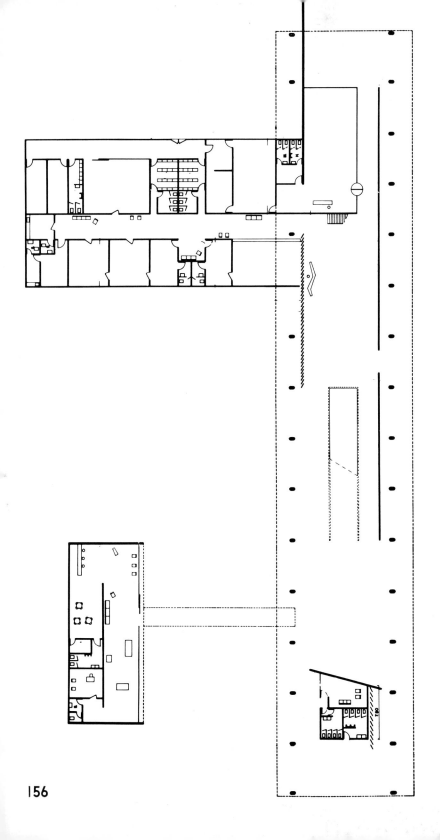

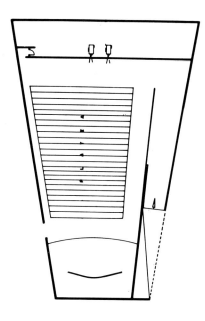

The ground floor plan on this page contains the administrative and health offices (upper left). With the exception of the library (top), the ramp (center) and toilets (bottom), most of the area under the classrooms is free in order to provide sheltered recess grounds. The students' club consists of a lounge in the front and a refreshment canteen in the rear. On the opposite page is the second floor plan with 30 classrooms, located on both sides of the building. The ramp, lounging space, toilets and locker rooms occupy the central area. Cross-ventilation for classrooms is obtained from above the corridor ceiling.

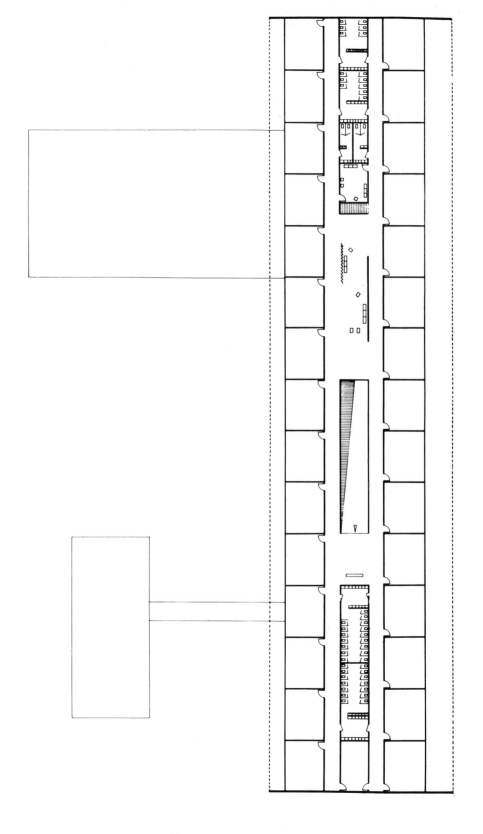

Construction pictures of the school taken in the summer of 1955. In spite of the absence of landscaping it is possible to see that the 1st floor is an integral part of the grounds. The walls on the 2nd floor, which divide the classrooms, are of reinforced concrete and participate in the structural scheme. Below: the auditorium, after the concrete was poured and the lower forms taken out, begins to have a recognizable shape.

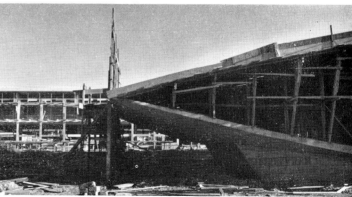

PART III

tasks

Variations on preceding themes make up the works included in this section. An architect's activity in answering a number of demands made upon him is not always spontaneous nor does it take the form of a prime approach to a problem; more often it is a question of developing a solution from within the frame of the architect's cultural horizons. Thus, what in a sense is considered "current business" by those who see in architecture a livelihood and not a dedication, receives here the grace of an active imagination and the engagement of a live interest. It is not then a paradox to say that the "minor works" should present the very climate in which the designer's creative potential could be understood.

1953. Housing facilities for the Aeronautical Training Center at São Jose dos Campos. Twenty row houses form a block roughly 590 ft. long by 60 ft. wide. With a visual pattern comprising two units, an impression is given that ten rather than twenty dwellings are in each row. The alternating solid and perforated screen walls between dwelling units, the planting in the front yards, and the play of light and shadow from the overhead screens break successfully the usual monotony of row housing. For additional housing facilities and general layout plan see the previously published volume, *The Work of Oscar Niemeyer*, pages 160-177.

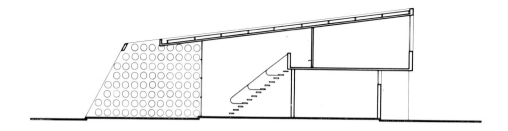

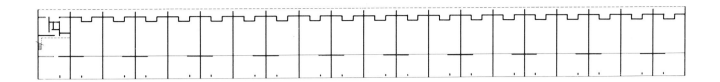

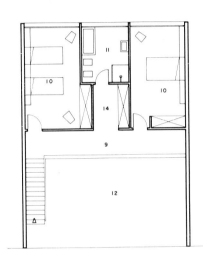

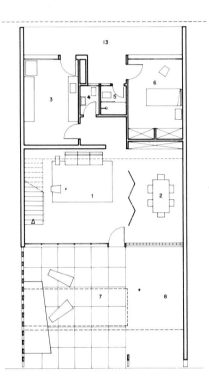

Each dwelling unit has a front terrace, 7, a portion of which is covered, 8; a service porch in the rear, 13; a story-and-a-half-high living room, 1; a dining recess, 2; kitchen, 3; maid's room and bath, 5, 6; all are on the ground floor level. Stairs from the living room lead to a balcony and to two bed rooms and a bath. The section on the opposite page shows the economical disposition of the total building volume.

Housing facilities at São Jose dos Campos.
Sixteen dwelling units of a larger type are included in this block. Although the second floor presents a continuous frontage reminiscent of a balustrade, the ground floor is interrupted between two consecutive units by T-shaped landscaped terraces; thus, the extremely long block offers less visual obstruction and implies less regimentation and depersonalization of the dwellers than its dimensions may suggest. Children in the picture on the right prove the successful scale of this building in spite of its gigantic size.

165

As in the preceding row houses, the living and dining room is one and a half stories high; three bed rooms, accessible from a balcony, are located directly above the front porch. The living room is open to the garden on the side and to the front porch. Left: a view of the end unit. On opposite page: the living room corner under the balcony, facing the porch.

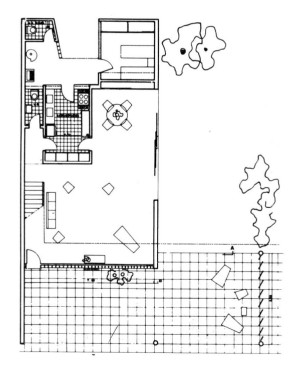

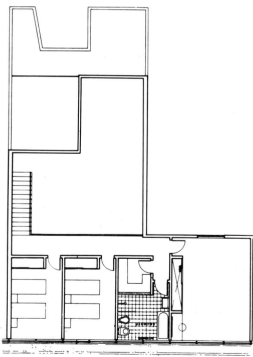

1955. Headquarters for the Foundation Getulio Vargas, approved preliminary project. Two blocks of buildings, opposite each other and linked at the 2nd-floor level by a low structure, occupy but a minimum portion of the lot, which is completely free at ground level. The unit on the left with the one-story link are planned for the Foundation's headquarters, and on the right a rental unit with small apartments is provided as an investment. While planning for the Foundation, the architect made an effort to develop a broader pattern for the urbanization of Botafogo Beach by which a maximum of the natural amenities would be preserved. On opposite page, right, 1, 2 and 3 are discarded schemes forming pockets of continuous wall barriers. The proposed solution (directly under) consists of a row of parallel, equidistant buildings, all of the same height and with their narrow sides facing the beach. The silhouette of the hilly background is thus preserved, and a semidirect view of the shore may be enjoyed from the buildings, the alignment of which is guided by the contour of the shoreline.

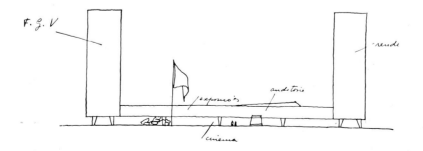

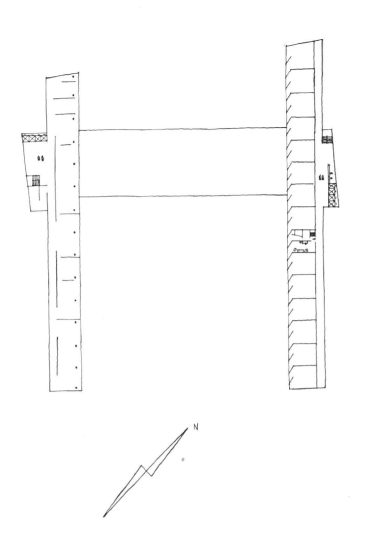

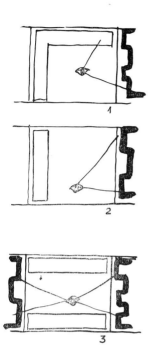

N

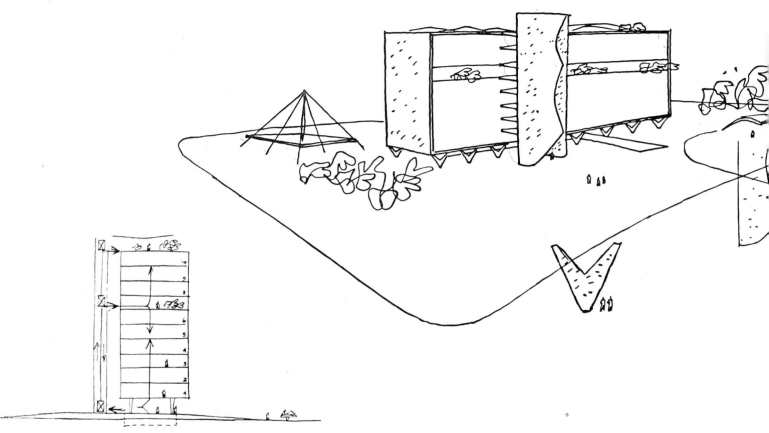

1955. Housing units for the 1957 International Reconstruction Fair at Berlin. Not only will the Fair inform the building trades of the most recent technical possibilities and make the public aware of a new, postwar modus vivendi, but also, at the end of the exhibition period, the whole undertaking will be inhabited and become a permanent part of Berlin's Hansa district. Fifteen architects were invited to participate in this "housing fair," each one contributing a personal approach to mass dwelling. The major characteristics of Niemeyer's project were established while the architect was in Berlin for two weeks during February of 1955; very few modifications took place in the final project which appears on these pages. The scheme consists of nine floors of one-level dwelling units with cross-ventilation; the ground floor, the 8th floor and the roof are given over to public recreational fa-

cilities, which, according to the architect, can only justify the reason for having multiple housing units. A rather complicated system of vertical circulation has been developed, partly for reasons of economy and partly on account of the architect's wish to provide for the dwellers a maximum privacy; as one landing serves only two apartments there is a need for a total of five staircases in the building. A semi-detached tower contains two elevators and a ramp serving only basement, ground floor, 8th floor and roof. The dwellers have the choice of walking up or down a number of flights of stairs (section at left). The structural scheme is extremely simple: ten spans on the ground floor with a length of 24 ft. 7$\frac{1}{4}$ in. and a cross span of 39 ft. 4$\frac{3}{4}$ in. with cantilevered parts of 6 ft. 7$\frac{1}{4}$ in. and 4 ft. 10$\frac{3}{4}$ in. On the upper floors there are twenty spans of 12 ft. 3$\frac{1}{2}$ in., and, consequently, lighter structural members.

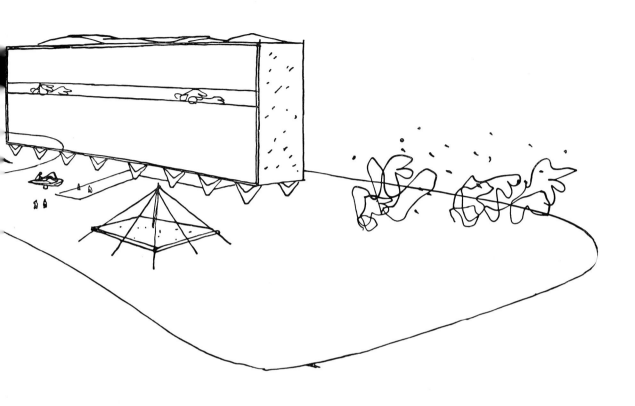

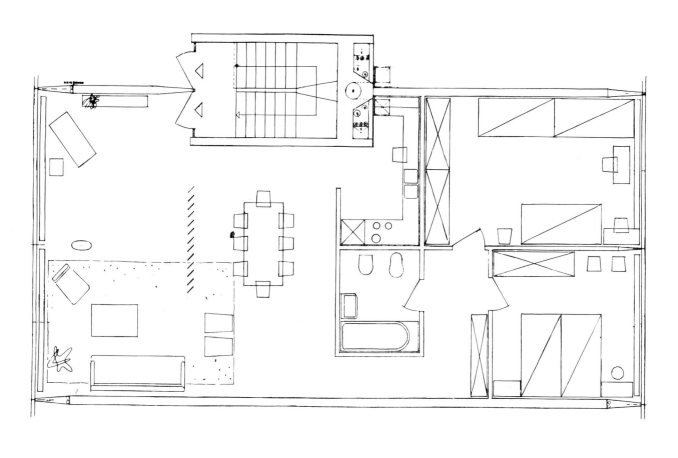

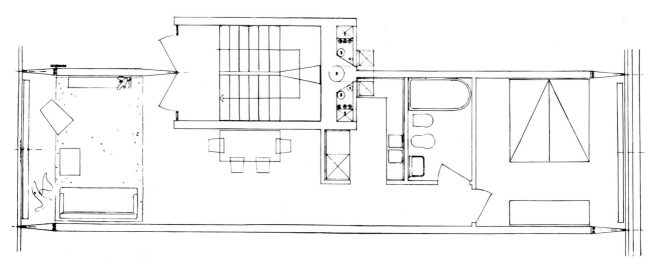

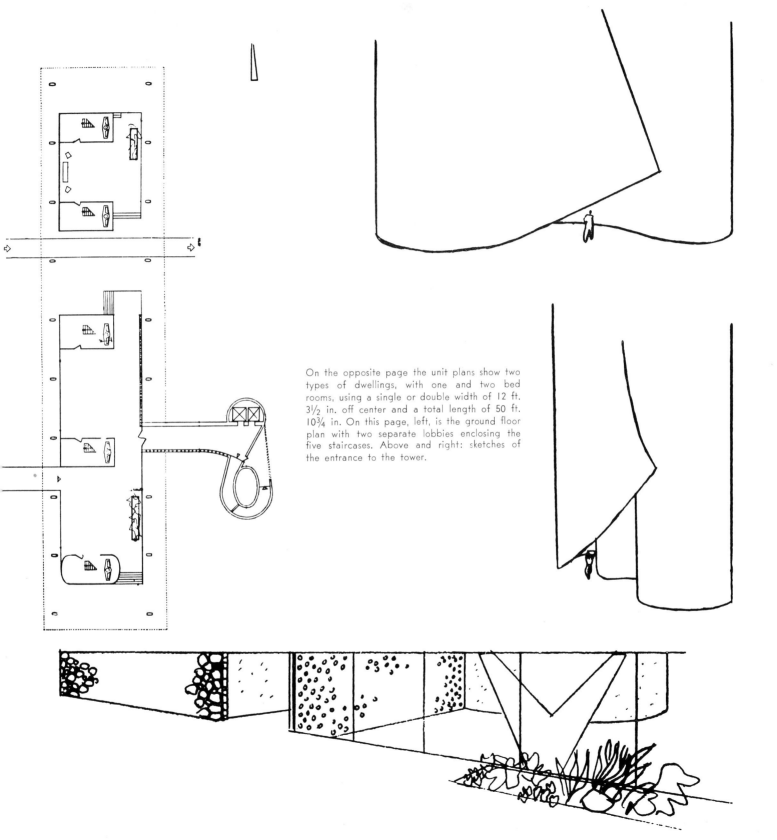

On the opposite page the unit plans show two types of dwellings, with one and two bed rooms, using a single or double width of 12 ft. 3½ in. off center and a total length of 50 ft. 10¾ in. On this page, left, is the ground floor plan with two separate lobbies enclosing the five staircases. Above and right: sketches of the entrance to the tower.

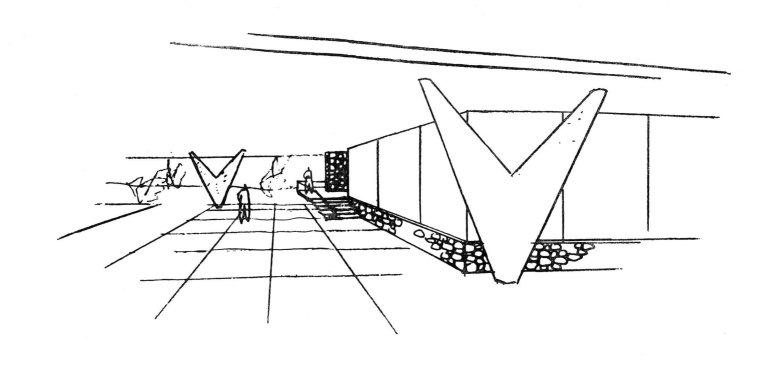

Interior-exterior views of the ground floor lobbies, raised from three to six steps above
ground, and of the entrances to the enclosed
staircases.

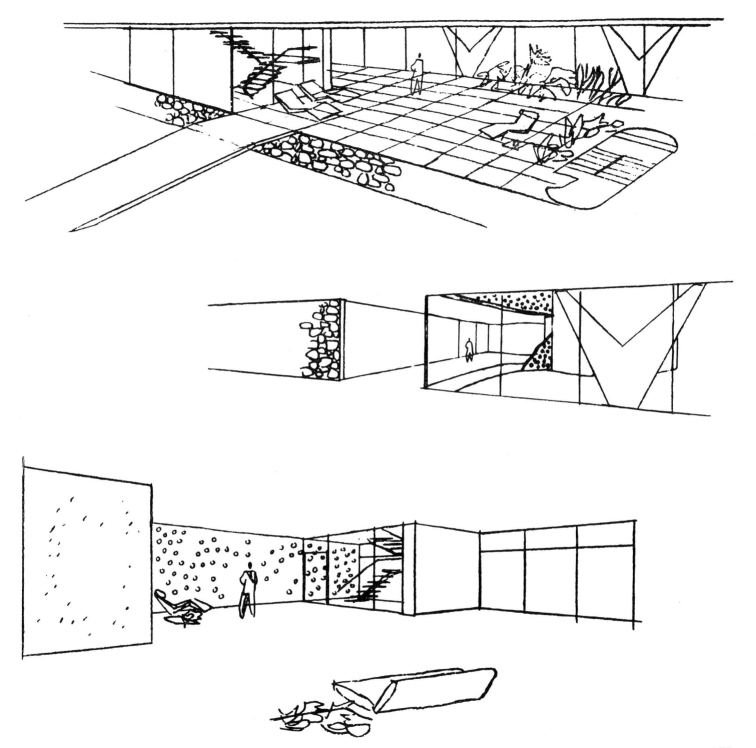

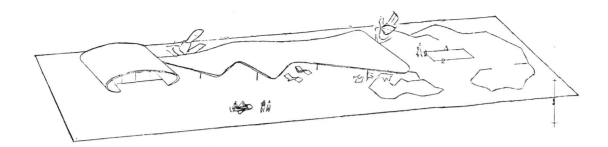

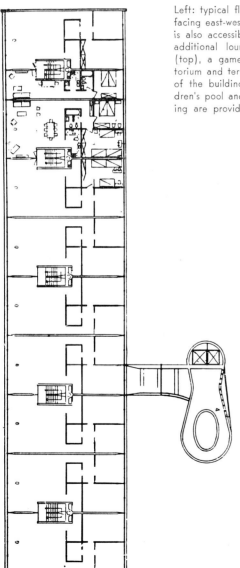

Left: typical floor plan with ten dwelling units facing east-west. Right: plan of 8th floor, which is also accessible from the tower and contains additional lounging space, a banquet room (top), a game room (bottom), a small auditorium and terraces on the east and west sides of the building. Above: a gymnasium, a children's pool and other facilities for outdoor living are provided on the roof.

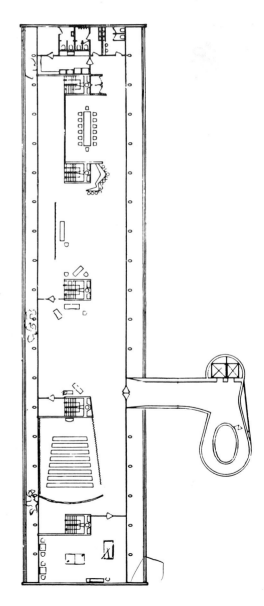

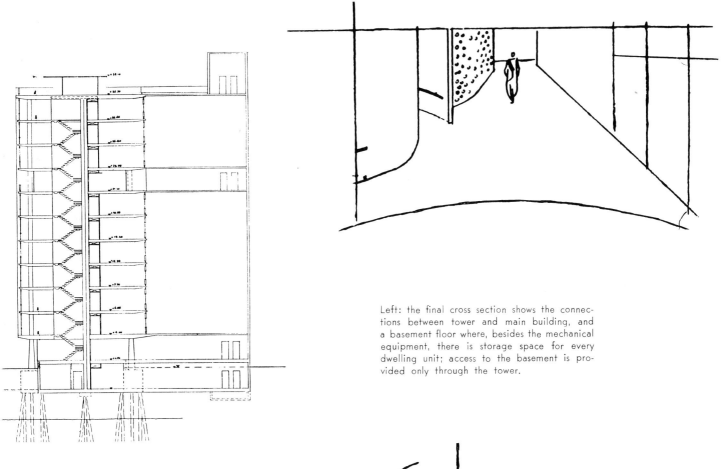

Left: the final cross section shows the connections between tower and main building, and a basement floor where, besides the mechanical equipment, there is storage space for every dwelling unit; access to the basement is provided only through the tower.

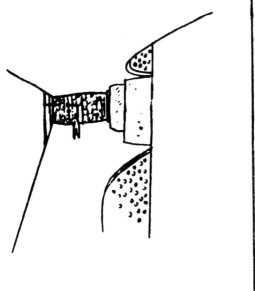

1953. Secondary school at Corumba, State of Mato Grosso. Structural Engineer: J. Alvariz. This educational building is situated in a town in western Central Brazil, near the Bolivian border, with a population of about 20,000. Unlike the previously shown schools with classrooms on a 2nd floor, here all facilities are provided for on one level. 1, the entrance; 2, the auditorium; and 3, the gymnasium; each has a different structural treatment and contrasts vividly with the repetitive elements of classroom units, 5, in the main building. On the right are located the administration and teachers' rooms, 4, at the end of the row of classrooms. A separate pavilion in the rear, accessible through a covered passage, contains toilets, 6; canteen, 7; and medical and dental offices, 8, 9.

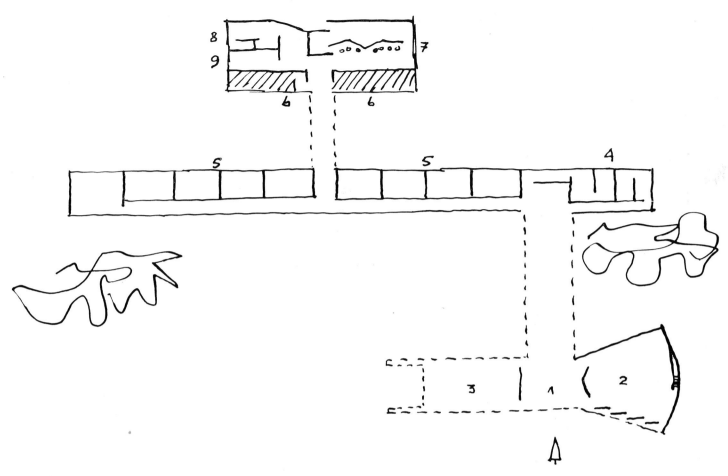

1952. House for Leonel Miranda at Rio de Janeiro. Structural Engineer: Joaquim Cardozo. Photography: Franceschi. A one-story house is raised to a proper level to secure a maximum of view. Two very gentle ramps, one from under the house and the other from the garden, provide the transition of levels. 1, living room; 2, dining; 3, study; 4, 5, service; 6, bed rooms and baths across the corridor; 7, ramp.

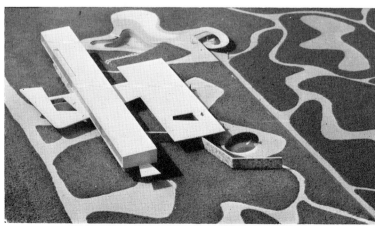

1953. House for B. Pigmatary at São Paolo. Associate Architect: Helio Uchoa. Structural Engineer: Joaquim Cardozo. Photography: R. Landau. Another attempt to achieve a background for total living in a modern fragmentary, "granular" world takes the form of a faraway island, reminiscent of the one described by Sir Thomas More. (For a previous similar project see *The Work of Oscar Niemeyer*, pages 188-195.) Of the three levels, the lowest is given over to a miniature amusement center (plan on opposite page): in the right wing, starting from the bottom, is a bowling alley, a gymnasium, a turkish bath, dressing rooms, a semisheltered swimming pool, a game room, a lounge, a canteen with bar and orchestra stand, and an outdoor swimming pool. In the left wing there is space for mechanical equipment, food storage, and a wine cellar.

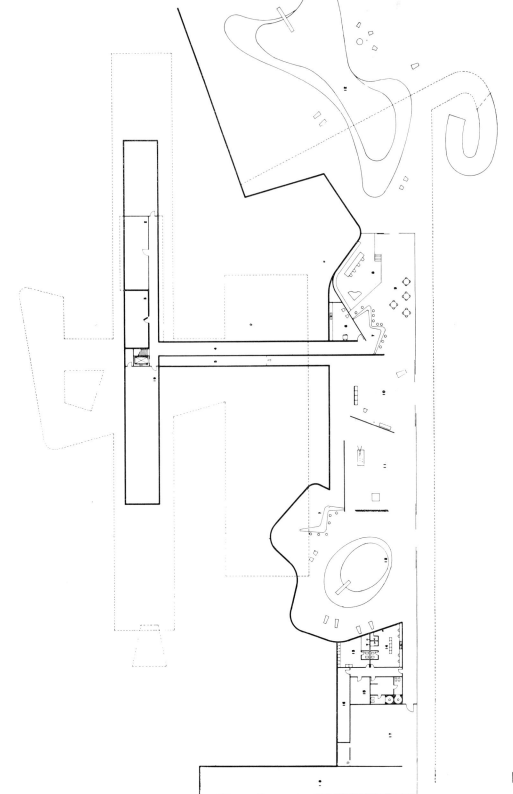

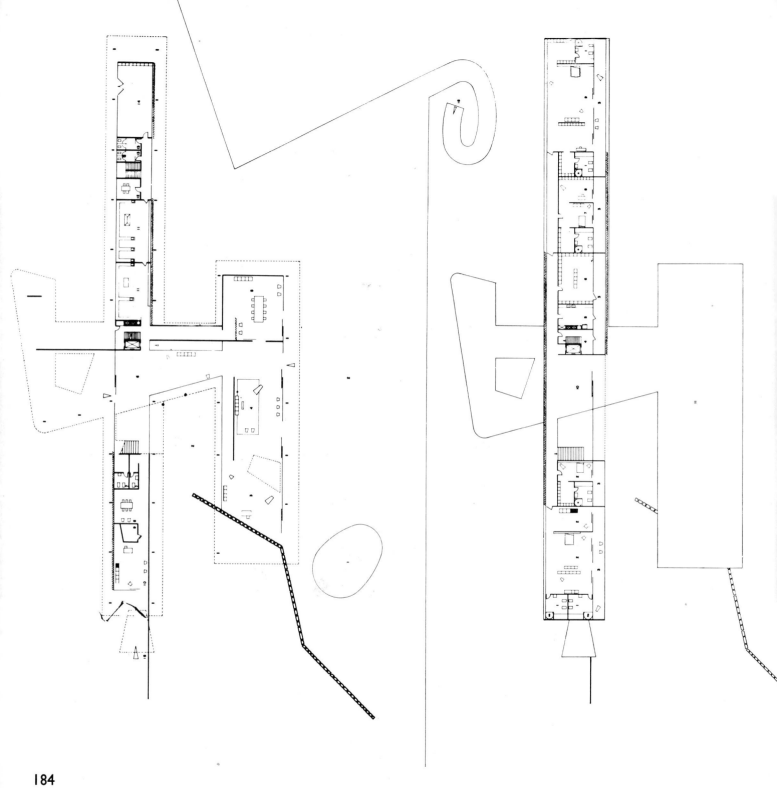

On opposite page, left: plan of the intermediate level (street level). In the right wing the living room and dining room overlook the terrace above the lower level; in the left wing the entrance hall, at the center, separates the kitchen and services (top) from a private study with separate entrance (bottom). Two ramps, one located between the two wings and another at the end of the terrace, connect this level with the lower one. On opposite page, right: plan of the upper level shows a guest

room with annexes at the bottom and a master bed room, also with annexes, at the top. On the right of the picture on this page the tunnel-garage can be seen disappearing into the hill. In spite of the total dimensions of the house there is an absence of a gargantuan impact. This is achieved by the way terraces and grounds are designed as a gradual continuation of the enclosed areas and the strong pattern of the gardens: it is an instance where a large element disappears within a still larger one.

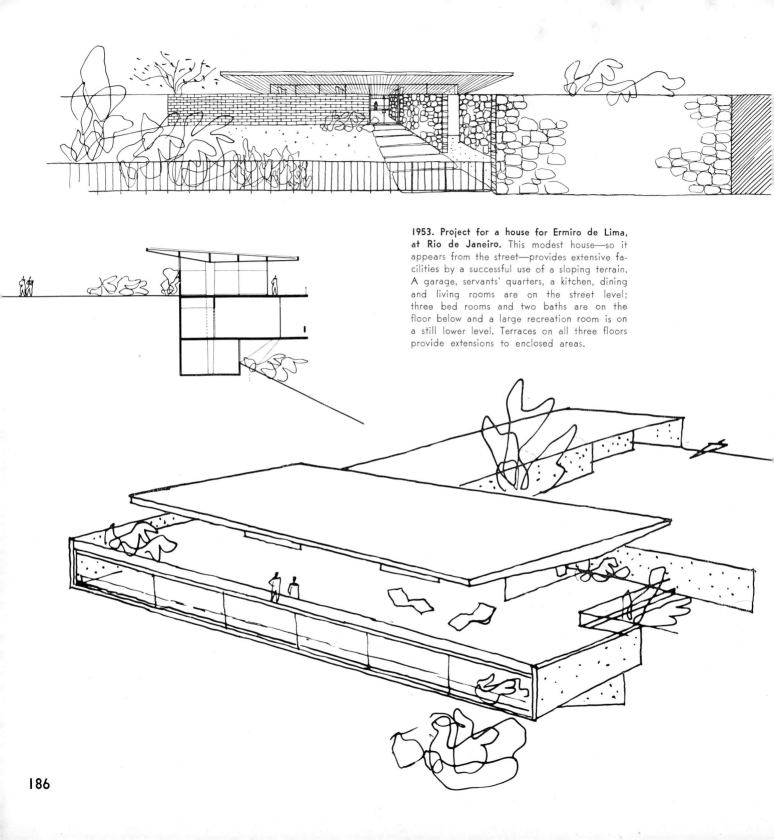

1953. Project for a house for Ermiro de Lima, at Rio de Janeiro. This modest house—so it appears from the street—provides extensive facilities by a successful use of a sloping terrain. A garage, servants' quarters, a kitchen, dining and living rooms are on the street level; three bed rooms and two baths are on the floor below and a large recreation room is on a still lower level. Terraces on all three floors provide extensions to enclosed areas.

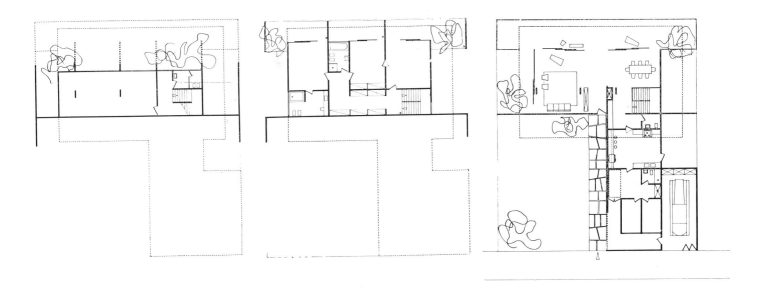
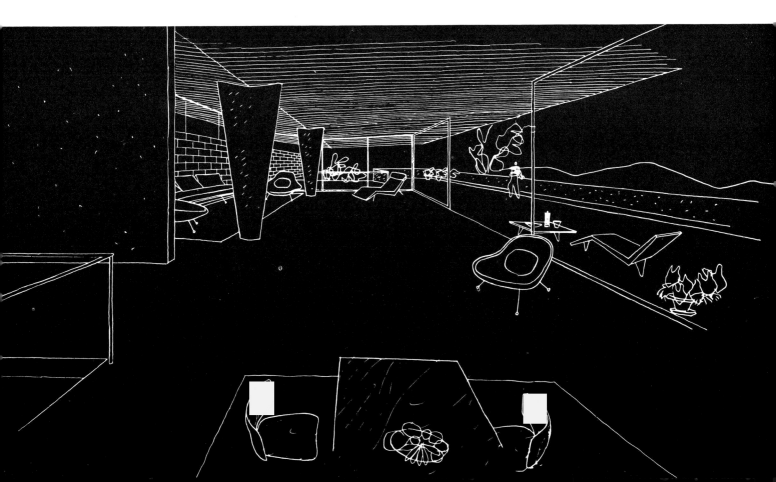

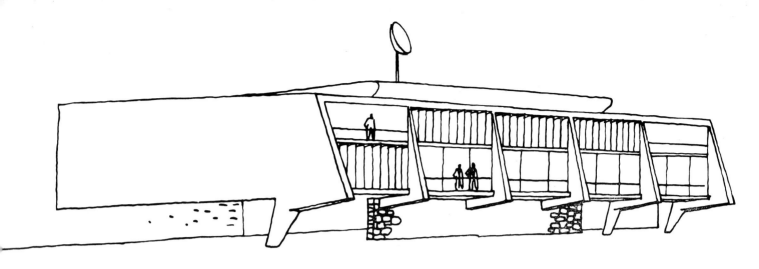

1952. Television station for "Diarios Associ-
ados" at Rio de Janeiro. Structural Engineers:
Pamplona and London. The station, to be connected with the new transmission tower on the
"Sugarloaf" mountain, has one medium-size
studio and two smaller ones; its facilities, because of the terrain, are developed on three
floors. 1, garage; 2, entrance lobby; 3, studios;
4, control room; 5, reception room; 6, dressing
rooms; 7, 8, shop and properties storage; 9,
lounge and observation; 10, administration; 11,
12, projection and viewing room; 13, labora-
tory; 14, upper part of the main studio.

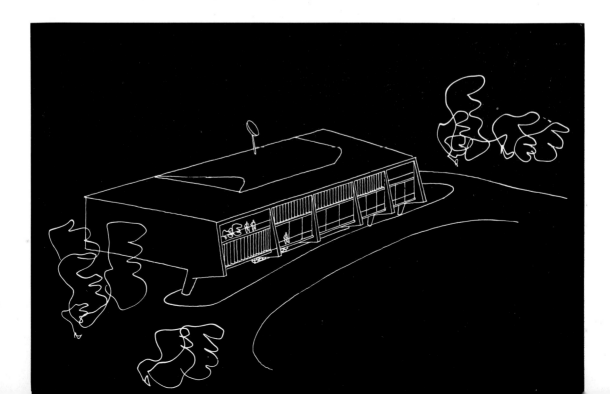

1954. Television station complex for "Televisão Rio." A preliminary study to include recreational facilities such as bathing and boating for the employees and talent is shown on these pages. A large production studio, circular in plan, and a five-story, square building of offices and laboratories, linked by a wide covered passage present the main pattern of the scheme; this pattern, in smaller scale and with minor variations, is repeated throughout. Here we have a bold attempt toward a sculptural synthesis of production facilities, which are more often seen as manufacturing problems with areas and volumes provided, improvised, or left for future adjustments. To an objection on the rigidity that such a scheme necessarily presents, it could be said, perhaps, that man's undertakings should perform as perfectly as possible at a given time and with the data at hand; any foreseeable growth of non-biological entities is an open speculation—more often an alibi for a designer's refusal to act under the term of flexibility.

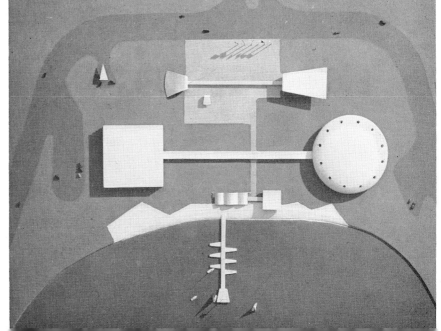

Building
Types
Index

Note: The previously published book, *The Work of Oscar Niemeyer*, is referred to here as volume 1; the present book is referred to as volume 2.

administration centers vol. 1, p. 180
airport terminal buildings vol. 2, p. 110
apartment houses vol. 1, p. 168. vol. 2, p. 18, 44, 170
arenas vol. 1, p. 45
athletic centers vol. 1, p. 34, 162

banks vol. 1, p. 142. vol. 2, p. 64
boat houses vol. 1, p. 128

casinos vol. 1, p. 70
churches vol. 1, p. 92. vol. 2, p. 116
clubs (social) vol. 2, p. 112, 122

dormitories vol. 1, p. 166

factories vol. 1, p. 224
fair grounds vol. 2, p. 125

homes vol. 1, p. 62, 116, 118, 124, 178, 188, 212. vol. 2, p. 68, 78, 180, 182, 186
hospitals vol. 2, p. 52
hotels vol. 1, p. 22, 104, 138, 218. vol. 2, p. 40, 100

monuments vol. 1, p. 214. vol. 2, p. 150
museums vol. 2, p. 82

nurseries vol. 1, p. 7

office buildings vol. 1, p. 48, 136, 142, 206. vol. 2, p. 60, 64, 168

pavilions vol. 1, p. 12. vol. 2, p. 134, 140, 142, 146, 150

restaurants vol. 1, p. 78, 128
row houses vol. 1, p. 170. vol. 2, p. 160, 164

schools vol. 1, p. 152, 165. vol. 2, p. 104, 154, 178
service stations vol. 2, p. 118
stadia vol. 1, p. 38
swimming pools vol. 1, p. 45

television stations vol. 2, p. 188, 190
theaters vol. 1, p. 112, 196

water towers vol. 1, p. 30
week-end houses vol. 1, p. 18, 20, 108, 202

yacht clubs vol. 1, p. 82, 132